ID0886646

Stress Research

Stress Research

Issues for the Eighties

Edited by

Cary L. Cooper

University of Manchester
Institute of Science and Technology

JOHN WILEY & SONS

Chichester · New York · Brisbane · Toronto · Singapore

Library of Congress Cataloging in Publication Data:

Stress research.

Includes index.
  1. Stress (Psychology) — Research — Addresses, essays, lectures. 2. Stress (Physiology) — Research — Addresses, essays, lectures. 3. Medicine, Psychosomatic — Addresses, essays, lectures. I. Cooper, Cary L. [DNLM: 1. Stress, psychological. 2. Job satisfaction. WM 172 S9157]
BF575.S75S7738 1983   155.9   82–11049

ISBN 0 471 10246 6

British Library Cataloguing in Publication Data:

Stress research.
  1. Stress (Psychology) 2. Stress (Physiology)
  I. Cooper, Cary L.
  616.8   BF575.S75

ISBN 0 471 10246 6

Phototypeset by Input Typesetting Ltd, London SW19 8DR
Printed in the United States of America

Contributors

Editor:

Cary L. Cooper
Professor of Organizational Psychology, Department of Management Sciences, University of Manchester, Institute of Science and Technology, Manchester, England

Robert D. Caplan
Senior Research Scientist, Survey Research Center, Institute for Social Research, University of Michigan, Michigan, USA

Margaret A. Chesney
Director, Behavioral Medicine Program, Stanford Research Institute International, California, USA

Hans J. Eysenck
Professor of Psychology, Institute of Psychiatry, The Maudsley Hospital, London, England

Stanislav Kasl
Professor of Epidemiology, Yale University Medical School, Connecticut, USA

Ray H. Rosenman
Senior Research Physician, Stanford Research Institute International, California, USA

Hans Selye
President, International Institute of Stress, University of Montreal, Montreal, Canada

Contents

Introduction **Cary L. Cooper**

1 The Stress Concept: Past, Present, and Future
Hans Selye 1

2 Specificity in Stress Models:
Examples Drawn From Type A Behaviour
Margaret A. Chesney and Ray H. Rosenman 21

3 Person–Environment Fit: Past, Present, and Future
Robert D. Caplan 35

4 Pursuing the Link Between Stressful Life Experiences and Disease:
A Time for Reappraisal
Stanislav V. Kasl 79

5 Problem Areas for Future Stress Research:
Cancer and Working Women
Cary L. Cooper 103

6 Stress, Disease, and Personality:
The 'Inoculation Effect'
Hans J. Eysenck 121

Index 147

Introduction

More than ever before *work* is not seen as the root of infinite satisfaction and fulfilment, but rather a source of stress, discontentment, and humiliation. Studs Terkel (1972) sums this up most succinctly:

> work is, by its very nature, about violence . . . to the spirit as well as to the body. It is about ulcers as well as accidents, about shouting matches as well as fistfights, about nervous breakdowns as well as kicking the dog around. It is, above all (or beneath all), about daily humiliations. To survive the day is triumph enough for the walking wounded among the great many of us.

This increasingly negative orientation to work is probably due to the fact that man no longer finds meaning or a sense of him/herself in the community, or as Freud (1962) once suggested, but which does not seem to exist today, 'his work at least gives him a secure place in a portion of reality, in the human community'. But the reason for this change of attitude is aptly highlighted by Terkel (1972): 'the planned obsolescence of people that is of a piece with the planned obsolescence of the things they make. Or sell. It is perhaps this fear of no longer being needed in a world of needless things that most clearly spells out the unnaturalness, the surreality of much that is called work today.'

It is because of the dramatic changes that have taken place in society over the last decade or two that work and life stress have become more immediate focal points of interest. This interest has reflected itself in an ever-increasing research orientation into occupational stress, the impact of life events, stress and disease, etc. With a burgeoning and disparate range of investigations being undertaken into the sources and manifestations of stress, it was felt that we should 'step back' and reflect on what should or needs to be done, that is, to focus on priorities or issues or problem areas of importance. To do this, the editor felt that he should call on distinguished researchers throughout the world, who have been involved with stress research for some time, and to provide them with a forum to express their own views about important issues, trends, and areas of need in the field of stress. The intention, therefore, was not to restrict the contributors to a set topic, but to issue them with a licence to develop their ideas about stress research; past, present, and future. Although the editor leaves himself open to the charge of 'overlap', 'duplication of ideas', or to criticism of 'lack of continuity among the various chapters', it was felt that the potential gain of allowing these most distinguished stress researchers 'free range' for their ideas would be greater.

This book is comprised of chapters that range from issues focusing on the individual, the environment, the person–environment fit, theoretical developments, and research methodology. We start the book with a revised view of the concept of stress, revisiting some of Selye's constructs. We then move to an examination of research on Type A behaviour and where it should go over the next decade. This is followed by an exploration of the effects of stressful life events on disease, i.e. the impact of the environment. The issues of the person–environment fit are explored in the next chapter, as are research topics into women at work and cancer in the following one. The direction of future research, theories susceptible to proof or disproof, and some findings which might suggest the direction of further research, are examined in depth in the final chapter.

References

Freud, S. *Civilisation and its Discontents*. New York: Norton, 1962.
Terkel, S. *Working*. New York: Avon, 1972.

Stress Research
Edited by Cary L. Cooper
© 1983, John Wiley & Sons Ltd

Chapter 1
The Stress Concept: Past, Present, and Future

Hans Selye
President, International Institute of Stress, University of Montreal, Canada

In our time, characterized by a rapid increase in the rate of medical and social developments, research on stress and adaption to change assumes particular importance in health and disease. We can no longer count on 'having finished our training' for our work or on 'having arrived at our goal' in society. Over fifty years have passed since I first conceived the notion of stress, and still, I do not consider my work on stress to be finished — far from it! I know very well that I shall never see the end of this study, for we are constantly faced with new ways of looking at almost every scientific problem. I think I can safely say, without exaggerating the vitality of this work, that it will go on forever, as long as biology and medicine exist, alongside the study of psychology and sociology.

When I first encountered 'the syndrome of just being sick' in 1936, I gave little thought to its psychological or sociological implications, for I saw stress as a purely physiological and medical phenomenon. The growing interest in this field, however, evidenced by the tremendous response of the general public to some of my nontechnical books, has made me realize that a knowledge of stress can benefit everyone regardless of educational background or profession.

Nowadays, everyone seems to be talking about stress. You hear it not only in daily conversation but also through television, radio, the newspapers, and the ever-increasing number of conferences, stress centres, and university courses devoted to the topic. Yet remarkably few people define the concept in the same way or even bother to attempt a clear-cut definition. The word *stress*, like *success*, *failure*, or *happiness*, means different things to different people and, except for a few specialized scientists, no one has really tried to define it, although it has become part of our daily vocabulary. Is it effort, fatigue, pain, fear, the need for concentration, the humiliation of censure, loss of blood, or even an unexpected success that requires complete reformulation of one's life? The businessman thinks of it as frustration or emotional tension, the air-traffic controller as a problem in concentration, the biochemist and endocrinologist as a purely chemical event, the athlete as a muscular tension. The problems they face are totally different, but medical research has shown that in many respects their bodies respond in a stereotyped manner with identical biochemical changes, meant fundamentally to cope with any type of increased demand upon the human machinery.

Stress is a nonspecific response of the body to any demand. In some respects, every demand made on the body is unique, that is, *specific*. Heat, cold, joy, sorrow, muscular exertion, drugs, and hormones elicit highly specific responses. For example, heat produces sweating; cold produces shivering; exertion, such as cycling up a hill at top speed, predominantly affects the muscles and the cardiovascular system. All these agents, however, have one thing in common: they increase the demand for readjustment, for performance of adaptive functions which re-establish normalcy. This rise in requirements is independent of the specific activity that caused the increase. In that sense, the response is nonspecific.

The nonspecific adaptive response of the body to any agent or situation is always the same, regardless of the particular stimulus; what varies is the degree of response, which in turn depends only on the intensity of the demand for adjustment. Thus, it is immaterial whether the stress-producing factor — or *stressor*, as it is properly called — is pleasant or unpleasant. A game of chess, a kiss, pneumonia, and a broken finger all produce the same systematic reaction, though their specific results may be quite different or even completely opposite. While it is difficult to see how such essentially differing conditions can provide an identical reaction in the body, the truth of this has been experimentally verified beyond doubt.

The first thing one should then bear in mind about stress is that a variety of dissimilar situations are capable of producing stress; and hence that no single one can, in itself, be pinpointed as the cause of the reaction as such. In all forms of life, there are common pathways which must mediate any attempt to adapt to conditions and sustain life.

The Birth of the Stress Concept

I first thought of what I later called 'biologic stress' when I was a second-year student at the University of Prague. During the first two years of our curriculum, we were never confronted with a patient; we followed exclusively preclinical courses in anatomy, histology, and biochemistry. It was only at the end of the second year that the great moment arrived which is awaited with such anticipation by all students of medicine, that of being faced for the first time with a patient. I will always remember the first lesson of our eminent internist, Professor von Jaksch, one of the most famous haematologists of the period. The subject of his introductory lecture was diagnosis. He asked his assistants to bring him five patients, specially chosen from different services of the University Hospital, who suffered from completely unrelated maladies. In every case he could arrive at the correct diagnosis by merely asking questions and looking for specific signs and symptoms of disease. I was deeply impressed by the logic of his interrogation and the precision of his observations, based on many years of experience. Almost all the manifestations of illness which he examined and nearly all the questions he asked concerned diagnostic indices, the very existence of which was unknown to me. It was an awe-inspiring spectacle to see that medicine had progressed so far that it was now possible for an experienced physician to make a correct diagnosis in so many different cases, even without the use of any complicated instrumentation or chemical examination.

After my initial amazement, I had a sudden thought. Why had the professor not said a word about all those signs and symptoms of disease which were perfectly obvious even to me, without previous knowledge of practical medicine, and which even the patients must have recognized, for they were what induced them to seek medical advice? All five patients, whatever their disease (one suffered from cancer of the stomach, another from tuberculosis, yet another from intense burns), had something in common: *they all looked and felt sick*. This may seem ridiculously childish and self-evident, but it was because I wondered about the obvious that the concept of 'stress' was born in my mind.

An examination of sick people will reveal that they are all indisposed, look tired, have no appetite, gradually lose weight, do not feel like going to work, and prefer to lie down rather than stand up. Today, we say that they show nonspecific manifestations of disease. They all present a syndrome simply indicative of being ill. That is why I baptized this state that so attracted my attention as 'the syndrome of being sick'.

After Professor von Jaksch's demonstration of his abilities, I rushed, in all my youthful enthusiasm, to our professor of physiology, explaining my ideas and asking him permission to work on developing them in his laboratory during free weekends or after study hours. My reception was somewhat discouraging. The professor laughed and said, 'If a person is sick, naturally he looks sick. If you look at a fat person, you can say he is fat. What of it?'

That analogy is the key to my work because the two examples are not the same. It is true that a fat person looks fat; that is an obvious fact. But it is quite different to make the generalization that the most diverse diseases have certain characteristics in common; in other words, that there exists a stereotyped syndrome which characterizes disease as such.

During this whole period I was obsessed with the thought that there existed specialists in every branch of medicine — there were physicians who looked after diseases of the eyes, the ears, the joints — but no one had tried to specialize in the common and hence most important syndrome: that of sickness as such. I wondered why the already well-known methods of exact scientific investigation, of looking for quantitatively measurable biochemical, microscopic, or functional changes, could not be employed to clarify the mechanism of 'the syndrome of just being sick'. Once this mystery was solved we might even succeed in suppressing the stereotyped manifestations of illness in all patients, whatever the specific underlying cause of their particular malady. We might prevent the loss of weight, the feeling of weakness, and other less uniformly displayed but still quite common disease manifestations, such as generalized aches and pains, inflammation, or loss of energy. After all, we already knew that antipyretics could restore body temperature to normal in different kinds of fever and we had found that analgesics would diminish pain due to diverse causes. It seemed plausible, therefore, that treatment could be directed against the nonspecified manifestations, rather than against particular disease producers.

The General Adaptation Syndrome (GAS)

It was ten years later that I again encountered 'the syndrome of just being sick'. In the course of experiments with rats at McGill University, I learned that a variety of impure and toxic gland preparations produce a stereotyped syndrome, characterized by enlargement and hyperactivity of the adrenal cortex, atrophy of the thymus gland and lymph nodes, and the appearance of gastrointestinal ulcers. Further research showed that this triad and other simultaneously occurring organ changes can also be induced by heat, cold, infection, trauma, haemorrhage, nervous irritation, and many other stimuli. Some of these changes are merely signs of damage; others are manifestations of the body's mechanism of defense against these diverse agents. The entire syndrome, including its pattern of development in time, was called the *general adaptation syndrome* (GAS). The GAS is made up of three stages:
  1. *Alarm reaction.* The organism's reaction when it is suddenly exposed to diverse stimuli to which it is not adapted. I suggested the term *alarm reaction* for the animal's initial response, because I thought that the syndrome probably represented a general call to arms of the body's defensive forces. The reaction has two phases:
      (a) *Shock phase.* The initial and immediate reaction to the noxious agent. Various signs of injury, such as tachycardia, loss of muscle tone, decreased temperature, and decreased blood pressure, are typical symptoms.
      (b) *Countershock phase.* A rebound reaction marked by the mobilization of defensive phase, during which the adrenal cortex is enlarged and secretion of the corticoid hormones is increased.

(Most of the acute stress diseases correspond to these two phases of the alarm reaction.)

The alarm reaction, however, is evidently not the entire response. No organism can be maintained continuously in a state of alarm. If the agent is so drastic that continued exposure becomes incompatible with life, the animal dies during the alarm reaction within the first hours or days. If it can survive, this initial reaction is necessarily followed by the 'stage of resistance'.

2. *Stage of resistance.* The organism's full adaptation to the stressor and the consequent improvement or disappearance of the symptoms. The manifestations of this second phase are quite different from — in many instances, the exact opposite of — those which characterize the alarm reaction. For example, during the alarm reaction, the cells of the adrenal cortex discharge their secretory granules into the bloodstream and thus become depleted of corticoid-containing lipid storage material; in the stage of resistance, on the other hand, the cortex becomes particularly rich in secretory granules. Whereas in the alarm reaction there is haemoconcentration, hypochloremia, and general tissue catabolism, during the stage of resistance there is haemodilution, hyperchloremia, and anabolism, with a return toward normal body weight. Curiously, after still more exposure to the noxious agent, the acquired adaptation is lost again. The animal enters into a third phase, the 'stage of exhaustion'.

3. *Stage of exhaustion.* Since adaptability is finite, exhaustion inexorably follows if the stressor is sufficiently severe and prolonged. Symptoms reappear, and if stress continues unabated, death ensures.

Because of its great practical importance, it should be pointed out that the body's adaptability, or 'adaptation energy', is finite since, under constant stress, exhaustion eventually ensues. We still do not know precisely what is lost, except that its not merely caloric energy, since food intake is normal during the stage of resistance. Hence, one would think that once adaptation has occurred and ample energy is available, resistance should go on indefinitely. But just as any inanimate machine gradually wears out, so does the human machine sooner or later become the victim of constant 'wear and tear'. These three stages are reminiscent of childhood (with its characteristic low resistance and excessive response to any kind of stimulus), adulthood (during which the body has adapted to most commonly encountered agents and resistance is increased), and senility (characterized by loss of adaptability and eventual exhaustion).

The successful management of our limited capacity to adapt to life's demands seems to be synonymous with the very process of life. Our reserves of adaptation energy might be compared to an inherited fortune from which we can make withdrawals but to which there is no evidence that we can make additional deposits. After exhaustion from excessively stressful activity, sleep and rest can restore resistance and adaptability very close to previous levels, but complete restoration is probably impossible. Every biologic activity causes wear and tear; it leaves some irreversible 'chemical scars' which accumulate to constitute the signs of ageing. Thus adaptability should be used wisely and sparingly rather than recklessly squandered by 'burning the candle at both ends'.

Mechanism of stress

Discoveries since 1936 have linked nonspecific stress with numerous bio-chemical and structural changes of previously unknown origin. There has also been considerable progress in analysing the mediation of stress reactions by hormones. The identity of the alarm signals may be metabolic by-products released during activity or damage, or they may be the lack of some vital substance consumed whenever any demand is made on an organ. Since the only two coordinating systems that connect all parts of the body with one another are the nervous and the vascular systems, we can assume that the alarm signals use one or both of these pathways. While nervous stimulation may cause a general stress response, denervated rats still show the classic syndrome when put under stress; so the nervous system cannot be the only route. It is probable that often, if not always, the signals travel in the blood. Alternatively, perhaps no one substance or deficiency has a monopoly on acting as an alarm signal; instead, perhaps a number of messengers carry the same signal.

The facts which led us to postulate the existence of the alarm signals would be in agreement with the view that the various cells send out different messengers. In that case the messages must somehow be tallied by the organs of adaptation.

Whatever the nature of the *first mediator*, however, its existence is assured by its effects, which have been observed and even measured. The discharge of ACTH (adrenocorticotrophic hormone), the involution of the lymphatic organs, the enlargement of the adrenals, the corticoid hormone content of the blood, the feeling of fatigue, and many other signs of stress can all be produced by injury or activity in any part of the body. Some method must exist to send messengers from any cell to the organs which are so uniformly affected by all stressors.

Through this first mediator, the stressor eventually excites the hypothala-mus, a complex bundle of nerve cells and fibres that acts as a bridge between the brain and the endocrine system (see Figure 1). The resulting nervous signals reach certain neuroendocrine cells in the median eminence (ME) of the hypothalamus, where they are transformed into CRF (corticotrophic hormone-releasing factor), a chemical messenger. In this way a message is relayed to the pituitary, causing a discharge of ACTH into the general circulation.

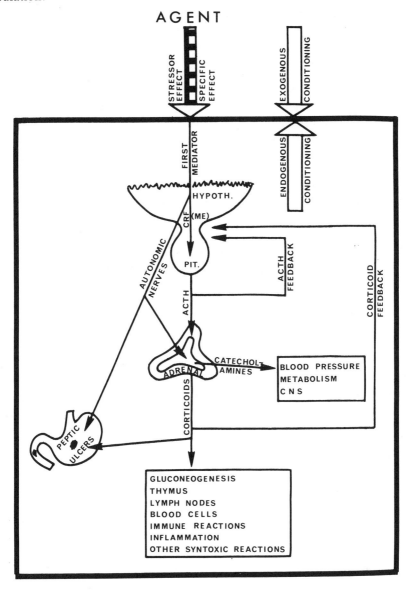

Figure 1   Principal pathways of the stress response

Upon reaching the adrenal cortex, ACTH triggers the secretion of corticoids, mainly glucocorticoids, such as cortisol or corticosterone. These compounds supply a readily available source of energy for adaptive reactions necessary to meet the demands made by the stressor agent. The corticoids also facilitate various other enzyme responses and suppress immune reactions as well as inflammation, thereby helping the body to coexist with pathogens.

Usually secreted in lesser amounts are the pro-inflammatory corticoids, which stimulate the proliferative ability and reactivity of the connective tissue, enhancing the 'inflammatory potential'. Thus, they help to build a strong barricade of connective tissue through which the body is protected against further invasion. Because of their prominent effect upon salt and water metabolism, these hormones have also been referred to as 'mineralo-corticoids' (e.g., desoxicorticosterone, aldosterone). The somatotrophic hormone (STH) or 'growth hormone' of the pituitary likewise stimulates defence reactions.

This chain of events is cybernetically controlled by several biofeedback mechanism. For instance, if there is a surplus of ACTH, a short-loop feedback returns some of it to the hypothalamus–pituitary axis, and this axis shuts off further ACTH production. In addition, through a long-loop feedback, a high blood level of corticoids similarly inhibits too much ACTH secretion.

Simultaneously with all these processes, another important pathway is utilized to mediate the stress response. Hormones such as catecholamines are liberated to activate mechanism of general usefulness for adaptation. Adrenaline in particular is secreted to make available energy, to accelerate the pulse rate, to elevate the blood pressure and the rate of blood circulation in the muscles, and to stimulate the central nervous system (CNS). The blood coagulation mechanism is also enhanced by adrenaline, as a protection against excessive bleeding if injuries are sustained in the encounter with the state of affairs eliciting stress. Innumerable other hormonal and chemical changes check and balance the body's functioning and stability, constituting a virtual arsenal of weapons by which the organism defends itself for survival.

In addition to the general adaptation syndrome, there develops in tissues more directly affected by stress a *local adaptation syndrome* (LAS). Whereas the GAS is the general or systemic response to a stressor, the LAS represents its local, or topical, equivalent. Obviously, nonspecific demands for adaptation may be limited to certain regions of the body (for example, inflammation, wound healing), but both specificity and localization are relative concepts: demands may be more, or less, specific in the type of response they require, or the region of the body that they affect. Thus, not only limited topical responses to diverse agents, but even nonspecific reactions primarily limited to certain systems (cardiovascular, nervous, RES), may be regarded as examples of an LAS.

In all these cases the LAS may cause a GAS. Thus, a nonspecific local inflammatory response may mobilize the hypothalamus–adrenal–pituitary axis for systemic defense if the demands are of sufficient intensity to require general adaptive reactions. The same is true even if the LAS selectively affects not a circumscribed body system, but the CNS, the immune system, or any other anatomical widespread but functionally separable and delimited entity.

It is somewhat disappointing that forty years after the first description of the alarm reaction we still know virtually nothing about the nature of the first mediator. All future studies along these lines should take into account that, despite the stereotyped nature of the stress response itself, we have no reason to believe that the first mediator is necessarily always an excess or lack of a single substance, or the result of nervous arousal. It must be remembered that nervous stimuli are certainly dispensable, since stress occurs under deep anaesthesia or after deafferation of the hypothalamus in mammals, as well as in lower forms of life that have no nervous system. It is quite conceivable that a stereotyped stress reaction can be produced through the most diverse means merely by deranging the homeostasis of biologic systems, which are notoriously labile. In this event, stress could be compared with fatigue or energy consumption, which likewise are nonspecific responses to any demand, be it pleasant or unpleasant. Also stress, fatigue, or energy utilization may be localized in any region of the body or generalized throughout more or less diffuse organ systems.

The stress response

The stress response has a tripartite mechanism, consisting of: (1) the direct effect of the stressor on the body; (2) internal responses that stimulate tissue defense or help to destroy damaging substances; and (3) internal responses that cause tissue surrender by inhibiting unnecessary or excessive defence.

Every agent that acts on the human body, from outside or from within, does certain things more than others. Those that it does more are relatively specific or characteristic for the agent, as compared to those that it does less. The latter, the nonspecific actions, may therefore be viewed as incidental side effects. But they are incidental only from the standpoint of classical medicine, which is always interested in the specific causes of disease and the specific cures with which to combat them. Stress research is primarily concerned with nonspecific actions. Whatever our point of view, we must keep in mind that, in actual practice, it is impossible to separate the specific from the nonspecific effects.

Stressors

The agents or demands that evoke the patterned response are referred to as stressors. Quite simply a stressor is that which causes stress. Stressors, it should be noted, are not exclusively physical in nature. Emotions, e.g., love, hate, joy, anger, challenge, and fear, as well as thoughts, also call forth the changes characteristic of the stress syndrome. In fact, psychological arousal is one of the most frequent activators. It cannot, however, be regarded as the only factor, since typical stress reactions can occur in patients exposed to trauma, haemorrhage, etc., while under deep anaesthesia. Anaesthetics themselves are commonly used in experimental medicine to produce stress, and 'stress of anaesthesia' is a serious problem in clinical surgery.

Syntoxic and catatoxic agents

The biochemical analysis of the stress syndrome showed that homeostasis depends mainly upon two types of reactions — syntoxic (Greek *syn* = 'together') and catatoxic (*cata* = 'against'). Apparently, in order to resist different stressors, the organism can regulate its own reaction through chemical messengers and nervous stimuli which either pacify or incite to fight.

Syntoxic stimuli permit adjustment to topical or systemic injury without directly attacking the aggressor. They create conditions for coexistence with toxic agents, either through passive indolence to them, or by actively stimulating the formation of a granulomatous barricade, which tends to isolate the irritant from the surrounding tissue. Through similar mechanisms, the syntoxic steroids also promote repair.

The systemic action of syntoxic agents is mainly of the 'life-maintaining corticoid' type; it is highly efficient in restoring the nonspecific resistance of adrenal-deficient organisms to normal, but then it reaches a plateau above which tolerance is not easily raised. Only in a few instances can syntoxic steroids increase tolerance far above normal because here the 'disease' is primarily due to active morbid reaction of the tissues, not to passive, direct tissue damage by the exogenous aggressor. In all these cases, though, it remains constant that homeostasis is achieved by adjusting the body's reaction to the damaging agent, not by destroying the latter.

Catatoxic stimuli act primarily by stimulating aggressive reactions which destroy toxic substances. On the other hand, they do not merely restore a deficient resistance to normal, but they are capable of raising it far above the norm. Sometimes this reaction defeats its purpose, because the products of metabolic degradation are more toxic than the original drug which was to be inactivated. Yet the response is still catatoxic since it attacks the aggressor.

Syntoxic and catatoxic reactions are the body's only defence against internal stressors. Although there are overlaps between syntoxic and catatoxic reactions, the distinction between the two categories is justified because, usually, individual hormones act predominantly by eliciting one or the other reaction form. Furthermore, available evidence suggests that the two types of defence are mediated through essentially distinct mechanisms.

When the stressor comes from outside, however, a third possibility exists; instead of putting up with the enemy or trying to destroy him, one may attempt to escape from the enemy. Walter Cannon spoke of the 'fight-or-flight response' of an organism to its environment: an emergency discharge of adrenaline quickens the pulse rate, raises the blood pressure to improve blood circulation to the muscles, and stimulates the central nervous system; digestion by the stomach and intestine is temporarily suspended; blood clots more quickly to protect against excessive bleeding if injuries are sustained during its encounter with the stressor; and the blood sugar is raised to supply additional energy to the muscles. These changes represent phases of the alarm reaction to stresss.

Cross-resistance and cross-sensitization

Early studies on the GAS already showed that several stresses applied simultaneously can have a cumulative effect. For example, cold and hunger decrease resistance to almost any stressor, and concurrent application of various drugs and/or physical agents may result in the summation of their stressor potency. In this case, it became customary to speak of 'cross-sensitization'. On the other hand, during or immediately following an alarm reaction produced by one stressor, there may develop a 'cross-resistance' against the damaging effect of another. In all these instances, it is very important to distinguish between specific and truly nonspecific or stressor effects. Certain agents may augment or diminish each other's toxicity merely because one increases or decreases the specific effect of the other.

Cross-resistance and cross-sensitization depend on a large number of factors, such as intensity and duration of the stressor action, associated specific effects of the stressors, genetic background, and species susceptibility. It is unlikely that all forms of cross-resistance or cross-sensitization rely on a single mechanism: a pituitary or adrenal hormone discharge could hardly be implicated in the types of cross-resistance that have been demonstrated after those organs have been removed.

There are no two identical individuals and it is not surprising that the same stressor may affect different people in different ways and to different degrees. We all know that in the same room some people can feel too hot, others too cold, and others just right. There exist many endogenous and exogenous factors that can selectively enhance or inhibit a stress response. 'Endogenous' refers to such internal factors as genetic predisposition, sex, age, early training, and previous damage to specific organs, while 'exogenous' applies to many external conditions operating at the time of the stress, such as treatment with drugs or hormones, dietary deficiencies, and the physical surroundings. Most exogenous conditioning agents may be regarded as acting through cross-resistance or cross-sensitization, as long as their effect is nonspecific.

Conditioning is understood as merely the establishment of conditions necessary for an agent to act. It can be positive if the conditions permit an action, or negative if they prevent it. Positive conditioning by corticoids has also been referred to as a 'permissive' action. The concept is by no means limited to the establishment of conditioned reflexes, although it includes these together with any other nervous, chemical, or physical factors that affect the body's reactivity.

The fact that the same stressor can cause different lesions in different individuals has been traced to 'conditioning factors' that can selectively enhance or inhibit one or the other stress effect. This conditioning may be endogenous (genetic predisposition, age, or sex) or exogenous (treatment with certain hormones, drugs, or dietary factors). Under the influence of such conditioning factors, a normally well-tolerated degree of stress can become pathogenic and cause diseases of adaptation. It then selectively affects those parts of the body that are particularly sensitized both by these conditioning factors and by the specific effects of the eliciting agent. This selectivity of damage is comparable to that in different chains, in each of which mechanical stress of identical tension will break the particular link that has become weakest as a result of internal or external factors. It was many years before it became generally understood that conditioning is not always positive, and certainly is not limited to corticoids. In fact, the entire concept of 'pluricausal diseases' is based upon the realization that certain morbid changes are not produced by one agent but by the simultaneous activity of conditioning and evocative factors.

Stress and Disease

Every disease causes a certain amount of stress, since it imposes demands for adaptation upon the organism. In turn, stress plays some role in the development of every disease; its effects — for better or worse — are added to the specific changes characteristic of the disease in question. That is why the effect of stress may be curative (as in the case of various forms of shock therapy, physical therapy, occupational therapy) or damaging, depending on whether the biochemical reactions characteristic of stress (for example, stress hormones are nervous reactions to stress) combat or accentuate the trouble.

Stressors can disrupt homeostasis in two ways: by being beyond our power of adaptability or by causing disease because there is a particular weakness in the structure of our organism. Think of a chain placed under tension — that is, physical stress. No matter what pulls on the chain and no matter in which direction, the result is the same — in other words, it is nonspecific. The chain is faced with a demand for resistance. Just as in the chain the weakest link (or in a machine the least resistance part) is most likely to break down, so in the human body there is always one organ or system which, owing to heredity or external influences, is the weakest and most likely to break down under general biological stress. In some people the heart, in others the nervous system or the gastrointestinal tract, may represent this weakest link. That is why people develop different types of diseases under the influence of the same kind of stressor. That is also why, strictly speaking, the pure stage of exhaustion is never reached. Before all adaptation energy is depleted, the weakest link breaks down, causing an immediate general collapse. Although I have performed over one thousand autopsies, I have not come across one case of death from old age, where all parts of the body, wearing at equal rates, have given in at the same time.

In typical diseases of adaptation, insufficient, excessive, or faulty reactions to stressors (for example, inappropriate hormonal or nervous responses) are at the root of the disturbance. Yet there is no disease that can be attributed exclusively to maladaptation, since the cause of nonspecific response will always be modified by various conditioning factors that enhance, diminish, or otherwise alter disease proneness. Most important among these are the specific effects of the primary pathogen, and the factors influencing the body's reactivity by endogenous or by exogenous conditioners. Hence, the diseases of adaptation cannot be ascribed to any one pathogen but to 'pathogenic constellations'; they belong to what we have called the *pluricausal diseases* ('multifactorial maladies') that depend upon the simultaneous effect of several potentially pathogenic factors, among which, sometimes, none alone would produce disease.

Even today there are many physicians who, in particular cases, have difficulty grasping the nonspecific aspect of the diseases of adaptation. Again and again, when faced with the interpretation of a peptic ulcer produced by a burn, they will quite justly emphasize that a peptic ulcer is a specific disease and that a skin burn is a specific type of injury affecting a particular region of the body surface. Similarly, if a patient develops a cardiac accident after a violent marital dispute, they will point out that both the result and the cause were specific.

Since this problem is so often misunderstood, it may be worth while to illustrate it by examples of well-known inanimate machines in which the common factor necessary for their function is the generation of energy which can then satisfy demands at an appropriate receptor. It is easy to conjecture, for example, that an electric bulb placed directly in contact with a waterfall will not produce light, and that an air conditioner will fail to cool or heat a room if it is only soaked in petroleum. All the effects that can be produced by the inanimate receptors depend upon energy derived from the diverse sources capable of furnishing it. Similarly, in biological terms, the diseases mentioned will not arise in patients exposed to the agents which were enumerated unless these do, in fact, produce stress.

Direct and indirect pathogens

Direct pathogens are those that act directly against the body irrespective of any vital tissue reaction. Thus, mechanical trauma, intense heat, and strong acids or alkalis will cause tissue damage irrespective of the body's response and, more particular, of the defensive reactions characteristic of stress. That these pathogens are really direct and independent of any vital activity is best demonstrated by the fact that they will affect a cadaver, which obviously could not develop morbid lesions as a consequence of its own vital reactions. Other examples of direct pathogens are endotoxins, spinal cord transection, and radiation. Their effects (fever, paralysis, the radiation syndrome) are not evident after death, yet they do act directly, to a large extent. It is true that the body's defensive reactions (particularly the stress response) can be elicited by direct pathogens in the living organisms as a secondary consequence of their specific effects. However, these specific actions are not, or only very slightly, influenced by the stress they produce.

Conversely, indirect pathogens act only, or predominantly, through the excessive or inappropriate defensive reactions which they elicit. For instance, emotional, immunological, and inflammatory reactions are primarily dependent upon such indirect mechanisms. The main purpose of inflammation is to localize irritants by enclosing them within a barricade of inflammatory tissue. This prevents their spread into the blood, which could lead to blood poisoning and death. However, there are times when, as in the case of allergy, the foreign agent itself is harmless and causes trouble only by inciting inflammation. Here inflammation is what we experience as the disease, and so the invader is an indirect pathogen. Again, the rejection of grafts and transplants represent an immunological reaction that evolved to protect organisms against potentially dangerous foreign materials, but in these cases the mechanisms are inappropriate and man can improve on nature by suppressing them.

Homeostasis and heterostasis

During the second half of the nineteenth century — well before anyone thought of stress — Claude Bernard pointed out clearly that the internal medium of the living organism is not merely a vehicle for carrying nourishment to cells but that 'it is the fixity of the *milieu intérieur* which is the condition of free and independent life.' Some fifty years later, Cannon (1935) suggested the designation *homeostasis* (from the Greek *homoios*, 'similar'; and *stasis*, 'position', 'standing') for 'the coordinated physiological processes which maintain most of the steady states in the organism', that is, the ability to stay the same or static.

What is meant by the 'fixity of the *milieu intérieur*'? Everything inside the skin and even the skin itself constitutes the internal medium. To maintain a healthy life, nothing within the body must be allowed to deviate far from the norm; if something does, the individual will become sick or even die.

One of the most characteristic features of all living beings is their ability to maintain the constancy of their internal milieu, despite changes in the surroundings. The physical properties and chemical composition of our body fluids and tissues tend to remain remarkably constant despite all the changes around us. For instance, if we are exposed to extreme cold or heat, our bodies will try to maintain a constant temperature. If this self-regulatory power fails, disease or even death may ensue. Homeostasis, the staying power of the body in an ever-changing environment, is therefore the all-inportant criterion of health.

Natural homeostatic mechanisms are usually sufficient to maintain a normal state of resistance; however, when the organism is faced with unusually heavy demands, ordinary homeostasis is not enough. The 'thermostat of defence' must be raised to a heightened level. For this process the term *heterostasis* (from the Greek *heteros*, 'other') as the establishment of a new steady state by treatment with agents that stimulate the physiological adaptive mechanisms through the development of normally dormant defensive tissue reactions. Both in homeostasis and in heterostasis, the *milieu intérieur* participates actively.

In homeostasic defence, the potential pathogen automatically activates usually adequate catatoxic or syntoxic mechanisms; when these do not suffice, natural catatoxic or syntoxic agents in additional quantities can be administered by the physician. These agents are not the same as, for example, antibiotics, which combat disease without the body's active participation. Heterostasis depends on treatment with artificial remedies that have no direct curative effect but can stimulate the production of unusually high amounts of the body's own natural chemical defences despite abnormally high demands, which could not be met without outside help.

The most salient difference between homeostasis and heterostasis is that the former maintains a normal steady state by physiological means, whereas the latter 'resets the thermostat' of resistance to a heightened defensive capacity by artificial intervention from the outside.

The Present Status of Stress Research

In this chapter it is impossible to give a meaningful sketch of all that has been learned about the structure of stress hormones, the nervous pathways involved, the medicines that have been developed to combat stress, and the diagnostic aids that this approach has offered. Nevertheless, the medical, chemical, and microscopic approaches to the problem have all been extremely successful. Since the time of the very first description of the GAS, the most important single discovery was made only recently. It showed that the brain produces certain simple chemical substances closely related to ACTH. These substances have morphine-like, pain-killing properties, and since they come from the inside (*endo*), they have been called endorphins. (I am especially proud that one of my former students, Dr. Roger Guillemin, was one of the three American scientists who shared the 1977 Nobel Prize for this remarkable discovery, although it was made quite independently of me at the Salk Institute.) The endorphins have opened up an entirely new field in medicine, particularly in stress research. Not only do they have anti-stress effects as pain-killers, but they also probably play an important role in the transmission of the alarm signal from the brain to the pituitary, and their concentration is especially high in the pituitary itself. They may in fact shed some light on the nature of the 'first mediator'.

Significant breakthroughs have also been made with the discovery of tranquilizers and psychotherapeutic chemicals to combat mental disease. These have reduced the number of institutionalized mental patients to an unprecedented low. Also worth mentioning are the enormously potent anti-ulcer drugs that block the pathways through which stress ulcers are produced.

Stress research, however, has not limited itself to the area of medicine. Increasing attention has been given to the development of psychological techniques and behavioural codes that anybody can use, after suitable instruction, to adjust to the particular demands made by his life.

Among these non-medical approaches are the relaxation techniques. We should spend a little time each day at complete rest, with our eyes closed, our muscles relaxed, breathing regularly and repeating words that are either meaningless or heard so often that they merely help us not think of anything in particular. This is the basis of transcendental meditation, Benson's relaxation technique, but there exist an infinite variety of other procedures. They have been given to us by religion, from the most ancient faiths up to the Eastern sages and contemporary theologies, and include reciting the litany or standard prayers in the quiet and elevating atmosphere of a house of worship, with tranquilizing music. These practices should not be underestimated merely because science cannot explain them; they have worked for so long and in so many forms that we must respect them.

More recently, biofeedback has added a great deal to the psychological approach. A number of highly sophisticated instruments have been developed that inform the user constantly about changes characteristic of stress within his own body, for example, blood pressures, pulse rate, body temperature, and even electrical brain waves. We do not yet have a scientific explanation for biofeedback, but if you learn to identify, instinctively or through instrumentation, when you are under stress, you can automatically avoid, or at least, reduce it.

Throughout history, innumerable great thinkers have approached the problem of health from the points of view of theology, psychology, sociology, and particularly medicine. Whatever the approach or technique they favoured, the focus has always been specialized. Only now are we really beginning to look upon health as an interdisciplinary problem. After all, we are thinking of the health of the most complex species known, and we will never arrive at a satisfactory solution if all of us take different and reductionist points of view. Of course, we have been very successful in improving health by research limited to molecular biology, electron microscopy, pharmacology, behavioural philosophy (including religious codes), sociology, politics, economics, or any of the other specialized disciplines; but each of us must avoid looking upon our particular field of expertise as the only, all-encompassing solution to human troubles and the only road to happiness. There is no point in understanding and repairing isolated parts of the human machine if the person considered as a total organism is deteriorating for lack of integration.

The concept of health as a question of body, mind, and spirit is receiving wide public recognition and importance. This holistic approach aims at enhancing our total well-being, in part through self-awareness. By learning to gauge our own innate energy, potential weaknesses, and strengths, we can all benefit from this approach. It requires a great deal of self-discipline and will-power, but we must not lose sight of the vital awareness that each of us is responsible for his or her own health and well-being. Otherwise, no matter what new treatments are developed, we will continue to be plagued by stress diseases.

Philosophic Implications

The philosophic and, particularly, the behavioural implications of research on the somatic and mental consequences of the stress and GAS concepts have stimulated a great deal of work, not only by professional philosophers and behavioural scientists, but also by theologians, writers of fiction and nonfiction, palaeontologists, motion picture and television producers, painters, and recently, even choreographers.

A clear distinction between the specific and nonspecific, as well as an awareness of the fundamental fact that specificity is always relative, are by no means limited to medicine and physiology. Our whole philosophy of life, and especially the justification of our behaviour, must take these factors into consideration. It has been a most stimulating experience to attempt the development of a code of behaviour based exclusively on natural laws, particularly those regulating efficient homeostasis. There appears to be a great similarity between the laws governing the maintenance of a healthy equilibrium, and those assisting us to achieve the satisfaction of success in reaching whatever goal we consider worth while, on both the somatic and the mental levels. Of course, our efforts represent only a beginning; much more work is needed to develop the applications of a natural code of behaviour to the innumerable problems encountered during a normal lifespan.

In formulating a natural code of behaviour, these thoughts are of fundamental importance. We must not only understand the profound biological need for the completion and fulfilment of our aspirations, but we must also know how to handle these in harmony with our particular inherited capacities. Not everybody is born with the same amount of adaptation energy.

Some general ways of dealing with stress include: (1) removing unnecessary stressors from our lives, (2) not allowing certain neutral events to become stressors, (3) developing a proficiency in dealing with conditions that we do not want to or cannot avoid, and (4) seeking relaxation or diversion from the demand. In addition, we must learn to recognize 'overstress' (hyperstress), when we have exceeded the limits of our adaptability; or 'understress' (hypostress), when we suffer from lack of self-realization (physical immobility, boredom, sensory deprivation).

The stress of life has four basic variations (shown in Figure 2), although in their most characteristic nonspecific manifestations they all depend on the same central phenomenon. Our goal should be to strike a balance between the equally destructive forces of hypo- and hyperstress, to find as much eustress as possible, and to minimize distress. Clearly, we cannot run away timidly from every unpleasant experience; in order to achieve our purposes, we must often put up with unhappiness, at least for a time. Here faintheartedness would in the long run prove even more distressing by depriving us of the joy of ultimate success. Unnecessary or too much distress — all distress, in general, that does not hold promise of eustress — is what is to be avoided.

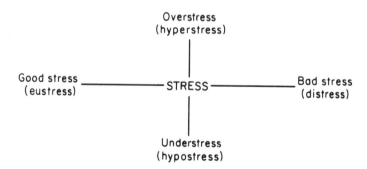

Figure 2   The four basic variations of stress

It is a biological law that man, like the lower animals, must fight and work for some goal that he considers worth while. We must use our innate capacities to enjoy the eustress of fulfilment. Only through effort, often aggressive egoistic effort, can we maintain our fitness and assure our homeostatic equilibrium with the surrounding society and the inanimate world. If we are to achieve this state, our activities must provide a capital to meet future needs. To succeed, we have to accept the scientifically established fact that man has an inescapable urge to work egoistically for things that can be stored to strengthen his homeostasis in the unpredictable situations with which life may confront him. These are not instincts we should combat or be ashamed of. We can do nothing about having been built to work, and it is primarily for our own good. Organs that are not used (muscles, bones, even brain) undergo inactivity atrophy, and every living being looks out first of all for itself.

Without the incentive to work out his role as *homo faber*, a person is likely to seek destructive, revolutionary outlets to relieve his basic need for self-assertive activity. Man may be able to solve the age-old problem of having to live by the sweat of his brow, but the fatal enemy of all utopias is boredom. What we shall have to do after technology makes most 'useful work' redundant is to invent new occupations. Even this will require a full-scale effort to teach 'play professions', such as the arts, philosophy, crafts, and science, to the public at large; there is no limit to how much each man can work on the perfection of himself and on giving pleasure to others.

People differ with regard to the amount and kind of work they consider worth doing to meet the exigencies of daily life and to assure their future security and happiness. In this respect, all of us are influenced by hereditary predispositions and the expectations of our society. Only through planned self-analysis can we establish what we really want; too many people suffer all their lives because they are too conservative to risk a radical change and break with traditions.

The way by which man can concurrently perfect himself and please others is altruistic egoism as expressed by the maxim of 'earn thy neighbour's love'. This motto, unlike 'love thy neighbour as thyself', is compatible with man's biological structure, but it can hardly be attacked as unethical. Who would blame someone who wants to assure his homeostasis and happiness by accumulating the treasure of other people's benevolence toward him? Yet this makes him virtually unassailable, for nobody wants to attack and destroy those upon whom he depends.

To live literally by the biblical command of 'love thy neighbour as thyself' only leads to guilt feelings, because it cannot be reconciled with the laws of objective science. Whether we like it or not, egoism is an inescapable characteristic of all living beings. But we can continue to benefit by the wisdom of this time-honoured maxim if, in the light of modern biological research, we merely reword it. Let our guide for conduct be the motto: 'earn thy neighbour's love'.

The Future of Stress Research

My work really has consisted of two parts. Most of my life I worked on what are called 'hard' scientific subjects — measurable things like microscopy, biochemistry, biophysics. It is only very recently that I suddenly changed my direction, because I felt that the future of stress research lies not here — that has been done already — but in two avenues of study which I consider particularly promising.

One avenue is to coordinate what knowledge we already have and to act as a catalyst between the many nations that have specialists who know a lot but who do not know of each other. That is why I founded the International Institute of Stress in Montreal. Ours is not a Canadian institute. It is situated in Canada, but we also have associations with various institutes throughout the world. Our library, the largest in the world on stress, contains 200 000 scientific articles and books which deal with stress. But that does not mean that people who should know about certain things really do know. They need a catalyst who brings them all together, who exchanges information.

The second major avenue that I think is promising is to try to apply the laws of Nature, which I learned about mainly in medicine and biochemistry as they apply to cells and organs, to human beings — to interpersonal relations, to international relations. Because curiously, the big laws of Nature are enormously generalizable.

I believe that new findings in medical science will provide many answers to humankind's everyday psychosocial problems. I do know that my own experience with health and disease has helped me to develop a very satisfactory code of conduct.

In essence, my code encourages people to lead purposeful lives, but to strive only for aims attainable to them as individuals. In this manner they satisfy nature's requirement that our adaptation energy and its machinery be used without, however, destroying it through overwork. The code is designed to achieve the pleasant stress of fulfilment, *eustress*, without the harmful consequences of damaging stress, *distress*. The point of the code is not to abolish stress but to master it. It is a matter of choosing, not an undemanding lifestyle, but a eustressfully rather than distressfully demanding one.

Reference

Cannon, W. B. Stresses and strains of homeostasisi. *American Journal of Medical Science*, **189**(1), 1935.

Chapter 2
Specificity in Stress Models: Examples Drawn from Type A Behaviour

Margaret A. Chesney
Department of Behavioural Medicine, SRI (Stanford Research Institute), Menlo Park, California, USA
Ray H. Rosenman
Senior Research Physician, SRI (Stanford Research Institute), Menlo Park, California, USA

Early in this century, scientific interest began to develop in the relevance of stress to health and disease. Despite its current prominence among scientific issues of popular interest, research in this field has been plagued with controversy. As Selye so aptly wrote recently, stress suffers from the mixed blessing of being too well known and too little understood (Selye, 1980). Some scientists assert that the stress concept has become too overgeneralized, encompassing both the stressor and the response to the stimulus, and that much of the available research is of questionable validity. Other investigators argue that the construct provides an important focus for research on behavioural factors in health and disease and that current problems in the stress literature can be resolved (Institute of Medicine, 1981). No debate could be more academic because the popular interest in stress is growing rather than diminishing and will demand clarifying information from the scientific community.

The last twenty-five years have witnessed an evolution of research on stress from the search for a *general* model of stress response to the recognition of the importance of *individual* response patterns to specific stressors. Stress research in the future will undoubtedly struggle with defining the complex, dynamic interactions among the environment, and individual perceptions of and physiological responses to that environment.

One model of this dynamic interaction based on literature on the Type A Behaviour Pattern (TABP) will be described in this chapter. To provide a backdrop for this model, landmarks in the recent evolution of stress research associated with Cannon, Selye, and Henry and Stephens will be briefly outlined in the first part of this chapter. Then, TABP will be merged with this backdrop, and research on TABP will be reviewed and integrated into a dynamic model of stress response.

Background to the Model

Early work sought to identify general patterns of response to stress. In 1929, Walter Cannon demonstrated the role of the sympathetic nervous system and adrenal medullary system (Cannon, 1929) in animal responses to threatening stimuli. To survive, animals must respond quickly to environmental life-threatening challenge. At times the appropriate reaction is to fight, while at other times the best reaction to such threat is to flee. Cannon called this the fight-or-flight reaction and showed that it is associated with activation of the adrenal medullary system, releasing catecholamines that result in increased cardiac output, arterial pressure, and heart rate. This work, highlighting the importance of one aspect of the adrenergic system, led to subsequent discovery of a broad spectrum of neuroendocrine responses to psychosocial stimulation.

Beginning in the 1930s, Hans Selye studied animals exposed to noxious stimuli such as cold, toxins, and traumatic injury and demonstrated the importance of the adrenocortical system in response to external stressors (Selye, 1950). In his early work, Selye injected rats with various impure and toxic gland preparations and observed such reactions as enlargement and hyperactivity of the adrenal cortex, atrophy of the thymus gland and lymph nodes, and gastrointestinal ulcers. Later, he discovered these same responses to other noxious stimuli and toxins and concluded that organisms have a pattern of stereotyped responses that becomes evident in response to 'nonspecific stimuli'. He termed this pattern the general adaptation syndrome (GAS), which has three stages. When an organism is confronted with a stress, the immediate response is alarm — the adrenocortical secretions rise with general sympathetic arousal. Following the alarm reaction, the stage of 'resistance' begins, and there is a decrease in adrenocortical secretions and a return to normal body functioning. If the threat continues, adrenocortical levels are again increased and may eventually be totally depleted, leading to 'exhaustion' and, in some cases, death.

In his book, *The Stress Without Distress* (1974), Selye argued that stress is essential to the life process and that alarm reactions are unavoidable. He characterized as positive the stress response and arousal that Cannon described. This type of stress, like that which an athlete experiences in a competition, must be distinguished from the harmful stress response when an individual is unable to cope and enters the final, exhaustion phase of the GAS.

One of Selye's major contributions was his recognition that stressors affect individuals differently based on many endogenous factors (e.g., genetic predisposition, sex, age, early training), and exogenous factors (e.g., drugs, dietary deficiencies, physical environment) that selectively enhance or inhibit individual stress responses. Moreover, he asserted that in the human body there is always one system that, according to external influences or heredity, is the weakest. It is the weak system that is first affected by stressors.

Although the two general response patterns identified by Cannon and Selye may initially appear to be distinct, recent research has demonstrated a close connection between the two. Henry and Stephens (1977), leaders in such research, have argued that the important factor differentiating between the two responses is the extent to which the organism can control the stimulus. In a number of elegant animal studies, these researchers demonstrated that, when organisms are challenged but given the opportunity of exerting control over the environment, they show increased activity and aggression and respond to the challenge with activation of the amygdala and sympathetic adrenal/medullary response pattern described by Cannon (1929). In contrast, when organisms are not given the possibility of such control, but instead are immobilized or defeated, they show a withdrawal response and the activation of the adrenocortical hormones described by Selye.

The model proposed by Henry and Stephens has received empirical support by the work of Frankenhauser, which shows sympathetic activation in situations permitting controllability by the person studied compared to adrenocortical activation in noncontrollable situations (see reviews by Frankenhauser, 1975, 1979, 1980). Frankenhauser has further demonstrated that situations, such as monotonous or aggressively competitive performance tasks, that require effort coupled with distress or negative affects are associated with activation of both adrenregic adrenocortical systems. Situations that require effort without distress, such as a simple reaction-time task, activate the sympathetic or adrenergic system and *suppress* the secretion of cortisol (Frankenhauser, Lundberg, and Forsman, 1980). According to Frankenhauser, the experiments like those discussed by Henry and Stephens (1977), in which animals are exposed to stressors while immobilized, reflect situations that involve distress without effort.

Situations that involve effort and distress as well as distress without effort can have pathophysiological consequences. This was demonstrated in a series of experiments by Corley and his colleagues in which six pairs of squirrel monkeys were confined to chairs for eight hours a day (Corley, Mauck, and Shiel, 1975). One of the monkeys had to turn off a light once a minute in order to prevent delivery of a shock to the tails of both monkeys. The monkeys with the responsibility for the light, that is, the monkeys in the situation involving effort (and probably distress) maintained physical activity and developed hypertension, indicating excessive sympathetic arousal, and also exhibited myocardial fibrosis. Of the six monkeys that were incapable of responding, and would be considered to have been in a 'distress without effort' situation, five collapsed with bradycardia and four died in asystole.

The recognition of the importance of controllability over stress indicates the roles that can be played by both the stressor situation and the individual organism in determining responses to stress. Lazarus (1976) pointed out that an essential factor in the individual's response to stress involves the person's appraisal of the stressor and the manner in which the person 'copes' with the situation. Thus, if a stressor does not outweigh an organism's ability to cope effectively, the effects of the stress will be minimized. Whereas when coping is ineffective and the stress prolonged, the effects of stress will be apparent. According to Lazarus, coping can involve two processes direct action, and palliation, including denial. Each of these processes can play a role in determining responses to and the effects of stress. Thus, rather than the general model of stress responses proposed by Cannon and Selye, the relationship of stress to disease now appears to be determined mainly by such aspects of the situation as the control it permits and by the characteristics of the individual. What are needed in the study of the relationship of stress to disease are models that: (1) characterize the processes by which organisms appraise and cope with specific situations, and then (2) identify the physiological response accompanying these processes that are linked to disease.

Type A Behaviour: A Dynamic Model of Stress Response

In the extensive stress literature, the Type A Behaviour Pattern (TABP) is one of the few individual psychosocial characteristics that have been shown to play a causal role in illness. In fact, the findings of research on TABP provide a clear example of a model of stress in which characteristics of the situation and person interact and result in the very neuroendocrine responses described by Cannon, Henry and Stephens, and others.

The TABP is a set of aggressive, ambitious, time-urgent, impatient and competitive behaviours that are often elicited by environmental stressors or challenges. The behaviour pattern is considered to be the result of a person–situation interaction in which a perceived challenging situation induces enhanced competitiveness, impatience, etc., in predisposed individuals. From the perspective of Henry and Stephens (1977), Type A individuals have been reported to be particularly challenged by situations in which their control is threatened (see Rosenman and Chesney, 1980). The primary responses of Type A persons to these situations is to struggle aggressively to exert and to maintain control over their environment (Glass, 1977). Thus, TABP is a characteristic style of responding to, and coping with, environmental challenge. The converse Type B Behaviour Pattern, originally defined as the relative absence of the behaviours described above, is increasingly perceived as an alternative style of responding to or coping with environmental challenges.

Type A and Type B behaviour are most accurately assessed by the Structured Interview (SI) (Rosenman, 1978; Chesney, Eagleston, and Rosenman, 1980) or by questionnaire scales, such as the Jenkins Activity Survey (Jenkins, Rosenman, and Zyzanski, 1974), the Bortner Scale (Bortner, 1969), and the Framingham Type A Scale (Haynes, *et al.*, 1978). The importance of the TABP particularly resides in its causal relationship to the incidence of coronary heart disease (CHD). Comparisons of the two assessment methods have consistently shown the SI to be a better predictor of CHD than questionnaires (Brand, *et al.*, 1978; Rosenman and Chesney, 1980).

Epidemiologic studies conducted during the past twenty years have firmly established a strong association between the TABP and CHD. The relationship between Type A behaviour and CHD was first demonstrated in the Western Collaborative Group Study (WCGS) (Rosenman, *et al.*, 1976). In this prospective study of CHD, a population of 3154 employed men was followed over a period of 8.5 years. One major finding of the WCGS was that the TABP, as assessed by means of the SI (Rosenman, *et al.*, 1964) administered at intake, constituted a 2 : 1 risk factor for CHD. Thus, the association was found to be independent of the effects of other risk factors, such as age, blood pressure, serum lipids, cigarette smoking, and parental history of CHD. Many other studies have confirmed the findings of the WCGS (Haynes, Feinlieb, and Kannel, 1980; Kornitzer, *et al.*, 1981; Rosenman and Chesney, 1980) and have shown that the TABP is also associated with recurrent myocardial infarction (Jenkins, *et al.*, 1976) and with the severity of coronary atherosclerosis (Friedman, *et al.*, 1968; Zyzanski, *et al.*, 1976; Frank, *et al.*, 1978; Blumenthal, *et al.*, 1978).

Type A Behaviour and Sympathetic Arousal

Type A behaviour is associated with the sympathetic nervous system arousal characteristic of the stress response described by Cannon (1929) and by Henry and Stephens (1977) based on their animal research. Individuals characterized as Type A have been shown to have greater elevations of catecholamines in response to environmental stressors than those exhibited by Type B subjects. This was first recognized by the finding that Type A persons have higher levels of catecholamines during the working day (Friedman, St. George, Byers, and Rosenman, 1960). In a laboratory study, Type A subjects were observed to have significantly higher levels of plasma norepinephrine than Type B subjects in response to a competitive task designed to be a stressor (Friedman, *et al.*, 1975). Similarly, it was shown by others that employed adult Type A male subjects respond with greater blood pressure and plasma epinephrine than Type B subjects when confronted by the challenge of playing a TV video game with an experimental confederate competitor (Glass, *et al.*, 1980). These findings associating Type A behaviour with excessive sympathetic arousal are most important because they are consistent with the mounting evidence that pathophysiological links between behaviour and cardiovascular disease appear to involve adrenergic activity which is associated with increases in blood pressure, heart rate, plasma free fatty acids and renin, all physiological factors predisposing to cardiovascular disease and its clinical manifestations (Herd, 1981).

A number of laboratory studies have shown that Type A subjects evidence significantly greater cardiovascular arousal to stressors than do Type B subjects. For example, Type A subjects tend to show greater heart rate and blood pressure responses to a variety of psychomotor and cognitive laboratory tasks (see Dembroski, *et al.*, 1979; Dembroski, MacDougall, and Shields, 1977; Dembroski, *et al.*, 1978; Jennings and Choi, 1981; Manuck, Craft, and Gold, 1978; Manuck and Garland, 1979). These differences are not unexpected, because the heart rate and blood pressure responses accompany the enhanced release of catecholamines in Type A subjects exposed to stressors.

Across studies, however, the response differences observed between Type A and Type B subjects are not entirely consistent. For example, differences in cardiovascular responses that are observed between Type A and B subjects in one age group may not be replicated in another age group. Dembroski and his colleagues (1979) found higher systolic blood pressure responses to the cold pressor test in Type A male students relative to Type B male students; others did not find these differences between Type A and B male students (Scherwitz, Berton, and Leventhal, 1978), adult male subjects (Ward, *et al.*, in press), or between Type A and B female students (MacDougall, Dembroski, and Krantz, 1981). Such inconsistencies and findings from subsequent research indicate that, as was the case with the early Cannon and Selye models, the stress-illness model in relation to Type A behaviour is more specific with regard to characteristics of the *situation* and of the *person* and his or her perceptions of the challenging situation.

Characteristics of the situation

The importance of the stressor situation in determining stress responses among Type A subjects has been demonstrated recently in a number of laboratory studies (see Dembroski, *et al.*, 1979; Glass, *et al.*, 1980; Goldband, 1979; Pittner and Houston, 1980). In each of these studies, properties of the stressor situations were varied in order to investigate the effect on response. In one such study (Dembroski *et al.*, 1979) male college students were presented with a cold pressor test and a reaction time task under two sets of instructions. One set minimized the challenge inherent in the task whereas the other set of instructions maximized the challenge. Differences between the Type A and Type B students were greater under the high challenge condition. This was particularly true for the cold pressor test, which did not produce significant differences in responses between the two types of students under the low challenge instructions.

Glass and his associates (Glass, *et al.*, 1980) also demonstrated the importance of the competitive nature of the challenge task in determining both cardiovascular and catecholamine stress responses. Under one condition, Type A and Type B subjects played a TV video game with an experimental confederate in silence (a 'no harassment' condition). In a second (harassment) condition, subjects played the same game with a confederate who criticized and berated them for their performance. During the 'no harassment' condition, there were no differences in stress responses between Type A and Type B subjects. However, during the 'harassment' condition, Type A subjects showed greater increases than did Type B subjects in heart rate, systolic blood pressure and plasma epinephrine. These and other Type A behaviour and stress response studies confirm early observations that Type A individuals do not respond to all situations as relevant stressors, and that it is only when the properties of the stressor situation are perceived as such that the Type A is so challenged that heightened cardiovascular responses are observed. These responses, mediated as they are by sympathetic nervous system arousal, may contribute to the higher relative risk for CHD that is associated with the TABP.

Characteristics of the person

Specific components or characteristics of Type A individuals may enhance or even inhibit their responses to stressors. The initial definition of the TABP was multidimensional (Rosenman, *et al.*, 1964). There is suggested evidence that some components of the behaviour pattern are more strongly causally associated with CHD than others. For example, potential for hostility, vigorous voice stylistics, competitiveness, and impatience significantly discriminated in the WCGS between subjects who developed CHD and those who did not (Matthews, *et al.*, 1977). In research examining components of TABP as well as responses to stressors, potential for hostility has correlated significantly with enhanced cardiovascular arousal only in Type A subjects (Dembroski, *et al.*, 1979; Dembroski, MacDougall and Lushene, 1979; Dembroski, *et al.*, 1978). Furthermore, Type A subjects with relatively high levels of potential for hostility show cardiovascular arousal to tasks under both minimal and maximum challenge instruction conditions (Dembroski, *et al.*, 1979).

The importance of characteristics of the person in determining stress responses to environmental challenge has been pointed out by research on

Type A behaviour among women. Although it also has been shown to be a risk factor for CHD in women (Haynes, *et al.*, 1980, Review Panel, 1981), responses of Type A and Type B females to laboratory stressors do not show the same pattern of differences as those found with Type A and Type B males. In a replication of the study varying the extent of challenge in instructions, Dembroski and his colleagues (MacDougall, Dembroski, and Krantz, 1981) found that, regardless of Type A behaviour ratings, females showed less cardiovascular responses than males to the reaction-time task, but not to the cold pressor test. Moreover, there were no differences in response between Type A and Type B females, with the exception that those Type A subjects who also were rated high on potential for hostility responded with significantly greater systolic blood pressure changes than did both the Type B subjects and the Type A subjects who were rated low in potential for hostility. Reasoning that Type A women may not perceive the psychomotor tasks as a challenge, Dembroski and his associates examined blood pressure responses among female students to a reaction-time task with monetary incentives, as well as to two interpersonal stressors, the Type A Structured Interview and a difficult oral quiz about events in American history. As in the previous study, there were no differences in responses to the psychomotor reaction-time task despite the monetary incentive. However, there were significant differences between Type A and Type B students in systolic blood pressure changes during the interview and the history quiz.

Similarly, Frankenhauser (1979) reports that, in general, women tend to respond to achievement demands with smaller increases in catecholamine excretion than do men. Sex differences in catecholamine excretion are generally minor during rest and relaxation, but appear in response to such challenges as intelligence testing and a colour–word conflict task. This pattern is particularly apparent for epinephrine but there is a similar trend for norepinephrine. This sex difference has been observed in laboratory studies of subjects from 4 to 35 years of age. In response to a naturalistic stressor, a six-hour matriculating examination, females did show significant increases in epinephrine secretion, but the rise was significantly greater for the males. Cortisol secretion showed a similar pattern of sex differences in response to this stressor. Despite these differences in arousal, the females' performance on all of these tasks studied was not lower than the males'. In fact, where differences in performance were observed, they favoured the women. Frankenhauser interprets these studies as suggesting that women may have a more 'economic' method of coping with stressors, and that this difference may have a bearing on sex differences in health. Thus, for example, higher rates of CHD in males may be related to their more frequent and more intense neuroendocrine responses to stress. There is also evidence that stress and coping responses may be learned at least in part. Women who have adopted a nontraditional female role, e.g., engineering, show increases in epinephrine to a cognitive-conflict task that is almost equal to those found for males in engineering (Collins and Frankenhauser, 1978).

These and the previously discussed findings again point to the importance of an individual's *perception* of the challenge inherent in a given situation in determining his or her physiological response to the situation. In general, men appear to perceive achievement tasks in the laboratory as more challenging than do women. Among males, the data suggest that Type A subjects may perceive laboratory tasks as challenging while Type B subjects do not. Among Type A subjects, those who rate higher on indices of hostility appear to perceive greater challenge in situations that are viewed by other Type A's as only minimally demanding. Moreover, these studies may reflect differences between the manner in which men and women, and Type A and Type B individuals, cope with stressors.

Coping Styles and Stressors

Recent studies examining cognitive coping strategies among Type A and Type B subjects indicate that Type A and Type B subjects may differ in their styles of *coping* with situations they perceive as challenging.

In one such study, subjects were questioned about their perceptions following a set of trials in which they were presented with a difficult concept-formation task. The Type A subjects' self-report indicated that they responded to the challenge in a more active or involved manner and resisted feelings of helplessness to a greater extent than did Type B subjects (Manuck and Garland, 1979). This style of coping is consistent with what Obrist (1976) has termed active or effortful coping that elicits pronounced sympathetic arousal.

Type A subjects employed greater suppression and denial than did Type B subjects in an experiment where they were either threatened with a shock if they made errors on a task, or were given feedback that their performance was not as good as that of other subjects (Pittner and Houston, 1980). Although the Type A subjects were using the cognitive coping strategies of suppression and denial, their physiological arousal during the performance feedback task was greater than exhibited by Type B subjects. Pittner and Houston suggest that 'an implication of the tendency by Type A individuals to use more denial is that it may lead them to endure stress longer and/or to endure higher levels of stress than Type B individuals'. (1980, p. 156) This concept is consistent with results from other studies, which showed Type A subjects to expend greater physical effort in a treadmill task, while acknowledging less fatigue than Type B subjects (Carver, Coleman, and Glass, 1976). The tendency to deny negative symptoms may account for delays in seeking medical care that have been observed in Type A individuals after onset of acute myocardial infarction (Matthews, *et al.*, 1981).

The scenario of denial in Type A persons and coronary patients is similar to the Human Function Curve theory proposed by Nixon (1981). This theory asserts that, in response to self-generated and environmental demands, coronary-prone individuals, such as those of Type A, deny fatigue in a struggle to achieve. Initially, the struggle is successful and achievement results. However, achievement is accompanied by rising aspirations and increasing demands. The end result is a downward spiral created by the fact that the harder one tries to maintain performance in the face of increasingly expanding goals and demands, the more severely health and ultimately performance deteriorate. This leads to escalating requirements for effort to maintain performance and culminates in exhaustion and ill-health, particularly CHD.

Conclusion

The most valid evidence to date of a link between stress and illness is provided by research relating the TABP to CHD. Efforts to identify the mechanisms underlying the risk associated with the TABP have underscored the importance of the interaction between specific properties of environmental challenge or stress and specific characteristics of the individual confronting the external challenge, including perceptions and coping styles. Just as early theories of stress looked for general models of environmental stressors and response patterns that are common across individuals, initially characteristics of the individual such as Type A behaviour and sex were thought inherently to lead to increased responsiveness to stressors. More recently, it has become apparent that it is the perception of the stressor by the individual and his or her selection of coping strategies that determine the type and degree of response to stress.

In the future, stress research needs to take into account the dynamic interaction between the situation and the person as it is now doing with regard to TABP. Rather than solely focusing on illness outcomes, this research needs to describe the *process* of these interactions in terms of environmental challenges, perceptions, and behavioural neuroendocrine, and physiological and behavioural responses to these challenges over time. Current developments in ambulatory monitoring now permit process measures of physiological variables and amplify the importance of developing process measures for the interactions between environmental stressors and behavioural variables.

Models like that being developed for Type A behaviour that capture the dynamic process of the relationship between various stress situations and individual responses to such situations are much needed. Such models would allow examination of such key issues as whether it is the *frequency* or the severity of stress and neuroendocrine responses that predicts disease, and whether variables such as social support or physical exercise mediate the effects of environmental stressors.

The ultimate value of these models will be in the design of primary and secondary prevention of stress-related illness. The more accurate our understanding of stress and its effects, the more precisely we can target our treatment and prevention, and the more effective will we be in disarming this contemporary problem.

References

Blumenthal, J. A., Williams, R., Kong, Y., Schanberg, S. M., and Thompson, L. W. (1978) Type A behaviour and angiographically documented coronary disease. *Circulation*, **58**, 634–9.

Bortner, R. W. (1969) A short rating scale as a potential measure of Pattern A behaviour. *Journal of Chronic Disease*, **22**, 87–91.

Brand, R. J., Rosenman, R. H., Jenkins, C. D., Sholtz, R. I., and Zyzanski, S. J. (1978) Comparison of coronary heart disease prediction in the Western Collaborative Group Study using the Structural Interview and the Jenkins Activity Survey assessments of the coronary-prone Type A behaviour pattern. Unpublished manuscript, University of California at Berkeley.

Cannon, W. G. (1929) *Bodily Changes in Pain, Hunger, Fear and Rage: An Account of Recent Researches into the Function of Emotional Excitement* (2nd edn). New York: Appleton.

Carver, C. S., Coleman, A. E., and Glass, D. C. (1976) The coronary-prone behaviour pattern and the suppression of fatigue on a treadmill test. *Journal of Personality and Social Psychology*, **33**, 460–6.

Collins, A., and Frankenhauser, M. (1978) Stress responses in male and female engineering students. *Journal of Human Stress*, **4**, 43–8.

Corley, K. C., Mauck, H. P., and Shiel, F. O'M. (1975) Cardiac responses associated with 'yoked chair' shock avoidance in squirrel monkeys. *Psychophysiology*, **12**, 439–44.

Chesney, M. A., Eagleston, J. E., and Rosenman, R. H. (1980) The Type A structure interview: A behavioural assessment in the rough. *Journal of Behavioural Assessment*, **2**(4), 255–72.

Dembroski, T. M., MacDougall, J. M., Herd, J. A., and Shields, J. L. (1979) Effect of level of challenge on pressor and heart rate responses in Type A and Type B subjects. *Journal of Applied Social Psychology*, **9**(3), 209–28.

Dembroski, T. M., MacDougall, J. M., and Lushene, R. (1979) Interpersonal interaction and cardiovascular response in Type A subjects and coronary patients. *Journal of Human Stress*, **5**, 28–36.

Dembroski, T. M., MacDougall, J. M., and Shields, J. L. (1977) Physiologic reactions to social challenge in persons evidencing the Type A coronary-prone behaviour pattern. *Journal of Human Stress*, **3**, 2–10.

Dembroski, T. M., MacDougall, J. M., Shields, J. L., Petitto, J., and Lushene, R. (1978) Components of the Type A coronary-prone behaviour pattern and cardiovascular responses to psychomotor performance challenge. *Journal of Behavioural Medicine*, **1**(2), 159–76.

Frank, K. A., Heller, S. S., Kornfeld, D. S., Sporn, A. A., and Weiss, M. B. (1978) Type A behaviour pattern and coronary angiographic findings. *Journal of the American Medical Association*, **240**, 761–3.

Frankenhauser, M. (1975) Sympathetic-adrenomedullary activity, behaviour and the psychosocial environment. In P. H. Venables and M. J. Christie (eds), *Research in Psychophysiology*. New York: Wiley, 71–94.

Frankenhauser, M. (1979) Psychoneuroendocrine approaches to the study of emotion as related to stress and coping. In H. E. Howe and R. A. Dienstbier (eds), *Nebraska Symposium on Motivation 1978*. Lincoln, Nebraska: University of Nebraska, 121–61.

Frankenhauser, M. (1980) Psychoneuroendocrine approaches to the study of stressful person-environment transactions. In H. Selye (ed.), *Selye's Guide to Stress Research*. New York: Van Nostrand Reinhold, 46–70.

Frankenhauser, M., Lundberg, U., and Forsman, L. (1980) Dissociation between sympathetic-adrenal and pituitary-adrenal responses to an achievement situation characterized by high controllability: Comparison between Type A and Type B males and females. *Biological Psychology*, **10**, 79–91.

Friedman, M., Byers, S. O., Diamant, J., and Rosenman, R. H. (1975) Plasma catecholamine response of coronary-prone subjects (Type A) to a specific challenge. *Metabolism*, **24**, 205–10.

Friedman, M., Rosenman, R. H., Straus, R., Wurm, M., and Kositchek, R. (1968) The relationship of behaviour pattern A to the state of coronary vasculature: A study of fifty-one autopsy subjects. *American Journal of Medicine*, **44**, 525–37.

Friedman, M., St. George, S., Byers, S. O., and Rosenman, R. H. (1960) Excretion of catecholamines, 17-Ketosteroids, 17-Hydroxycorticoids and 5-Hydroxyindole in men exhibiting a particular behaviour pattern (A) associated with high incidence of clinical coronary artery disease. *Journal of Clinical Investigation*, **39** 758–64.

Glass, D. C., (1977) *Behaviour Patterns, Stress and Coronary Disease*. Hillsdale, New Jersey: Lawrence Erlbaum.

Glass, D. C., Krakoff, L. R., Contrada, R., Hilton, W. F., Kehoe, K., et al. (1980) Effect of harassment and competition upon cardiovascular and catecholaminic responses in Type A and Type B individuals. *Psychophysiology*, **17** 453–63.

Goldband, S. (1979) Environme specificity of physiological response to stress in coronary-prone subjects. Unpublished doctoral dissertation, State University of New York at Buffalo.

Haynes, S. G., Feinleib, M., and Kannel, W. B. (1980) The relationship of psychosocial factors to coronary heart disease in the Framingham Study. III Eight-year incidence of coronary heart disease. *American Journal of Epidemiology*, **III**(1), 37–58.

Haynes, S. G., Levine, S., Scotch, N., Feinleib, M., and Kannel, W. B. (1978) The relationship of psychosocial factors to coronary heart disease in the Framingham Study: I Methods and risk factors. *American Journal of Epidemiology*, **197**(5), 362–83.

Henry, J. P., and Stephens, P. M. (1977) *Stress, Health, and the Social Environment: A Sociobiologic Approach to Medicine*. New York: Springer-Verlag.

Herd, J. A., Behavioral factors in the physiological mechanisms of cardiovascular disease. In S. M. Weiss, J. A. Herd, and B. H. Fox (eds.), *Perspectives on Behavioral Medicine*. New York: Academic Press, 1981, pp. 55–66.

ZmInstitute of Medicine (1981) *Research on Stress and Human Health*. Washington, D.C.: National Academy Press.

Jenkins, C. D., Rosenman R. H., and Zyzanski, S. J. (1974) Prediction of clinical coronary heart disease by a test for coronary-prone behaviour pattern. *New England Journal of Medicine*, **290**, 1271–5.

Jenkins, C. D., Zyzanski, S. J., Rosenman, R. H., et al. (1976) Risk of new myocardial infarction in middle-aged men with manifest coronary heart disease. *Circulation*, **53** 342–7.

Jennings, R. J., and Choi, S. (1981) Type A components and psychophysiological responses to an attention-demanding performance task. *Psychosomatic Medicine*, **43**(6), 475–87.

Kornitzer, M., Kittel, F., DeBacker, G., and Dramaix, M. (1981) The Belgian heart disease prevention project: Type A behaviour pattern and the prevalence of coronary heart disease. *Psychosomatic Medicine*, **43**, 133–45.

Lazarus, R. S. (1976) *Patterns of Adjustment*. New York: McGraw-Hill.

MacDougall, J. M., Dembroski, T. M., and Krantz, D. S. (1981) Effects of types of challenge on pressor and heart rate responses in Type A and B females. *Psychophysiology* **18**, 1–9.

Manuck, S. B., Craft, S., and Gold, K. J. (1978) Coronary-prone behaviour pattern and cardiovascular response. *Psychophysiology*, **15**, 403–11.

Manuck, S. B., and Garland, F. N. (1979) Coronary-prone behaviour pattern, task incentive and cardiovascular response. *Psychophysiology*, **2**, 136–42.

Matthews, K. A., Glass, D. C., Rosenman, R. H., and Bortner, R. W. (1977) Competitive drive, pattern A, and coronary heart disease: A further analysis of some data from the Western Collaborative Group Study. *Journal of Chronic Diseases*, **30** 489–98.

Matthews, K. A., Siegel, J. M., Kuller, L. H., Thompson, M., and Varat, M. (1981) Determinants of seeking medical care by myocardial infarction victims. Paper presented at Annual Meeting of the American Psychological Association, Los Angeles, California.

Nixon, P. G. F. (1981) The human function curve. Paper presented at the International Symposium on Psychophysiological Risk Factor of Cardiovascular Diseases. Karlovy Vary, Czechoslovakia.

Obrist, P. A. (1976) The cardiovascular behavioural interaction: At it appears today. *Psychophysiology*, **13**, 95–107.

Pittner, M. S., and Houston, B. (1980) Response to stress, cognitive coping strategies, and the Type A behaviour pattern. *Journal of Personality and Social Psychology*, **39**, 147–57.

Review Panel (1981) Coronary-prone behaviour and coronary heart disease: A critical review. *Circulation*, **63**, 1199–215.

Rosenman, R. H. (1978) The interview method of assessment of the coronary-prone behaviour pattern. In T. M. Dembroski, S. M. Weiss, J. L. Shields, S. G. Haynes, and M. Feinleib (eds), *Coronary-Prone Behaviour*. New York: Springer-Verlag.

Rosenman, R. H., Brand, R. J., Sholtz, R. I., and Friedman, M. (1976) Multivariate prediction of coronary heart disease during 8.5 year follow-up in the Western Collaborative Group Study. *American Journal of Cardiology*, **37**, 903–10.

Rosenman, R. H., and Chesney, M. A. (1980) The relationship of Type A behaviour to coronary heart disease. *Activitas Nervosa Superior*, **22**, 1–45.

Rosenman, R. H., Friedman, M., Straus, R., Wurm, M., Kositcheck, R., Harn, W., and Werthessen, N. T. (1964) A predictive study of coronary heart disease. *Journal of the American Medical Association* **189**, 103–10.

Scherwitz, L., Berton, K., and Leventhal, H. Type A behavior, self-involvement, and cardiovascular response. *Psychosomatic Medicine*, 1978, **40**, 593–609.

Selye, H. (1950) *The Physiology and Pathology of Exposure to Stress*. Montreal: Acta.

Selye, H. (1974) *Stress Without Distress*. Philadelphia, Pennsylvania: Lippincott.

Selye, H. (1980) The stress concept today. In I. L. Kutash and L. B. Schlesinger *Handbook on Stress and Anxiety*. San Francisco, California: Jossey-Bass, 127–143.
Ward, M. M., Chesney, M. A., Swan, G. E., Black, G. W., Parker, S. D., and Rosenman, R. H. Cardiovascular responsiveness to a series of challenging tasks in Type A and Type B adult male subjects. *Psychophysiology*, in press.
Zyzanski, S. J., Jenkins, C. D., Ryan, T. J., Flessas, A., and Everist, M. (1976) Psychological correlates of coronary angiographic findings. *Archives of Internal Medicine*, **136**, 1234–7.

Stress Research
Edited by Cary L. Cooper
© 1983, John Wiley & Sons, Ltd.

Chapter 3
Person–Environment Fit:
Past, Present, and Future[1]

Robert D. Caplan
Senior Study Director, Institute for Social Research, The University of Michigan, USA

> Our behaviour does not depend entirely on our present situation. One's mood is deeply affected by one's hopes, wishes and views of one's own past.
>
> after Kurt Lewin, 1942

Person–environment (PE) fit theory deals with how characteristics of the person and environment affect well-being. The predictive power of the theory, although encouraging, has not been impressive (see review that follows). As described below, some methodological problems may account for part of this state of affairs. Part of the problem, however, may be substantive and may have to do with an overly narrow focus on PE fit in the present time frame ('How good is the fit *now*?'). Based on this assumed weakness, an elaborated model of PE fit is described below that incorporates both past and future fit as stressors. The elaborated model deals with the person's perceptions of the past, present, and future in relation to the objective past, present, and future.

What follows is a brief review of basic concepts and hypotheses in PE fit theory, tests of the theory, and some methodological issues that are expected to persist even for the elaborated model. After the review, there is a description of the elaborated model and some hypotheses derivable from the model. The reader can expect a mix of derivation and speculation in keeping with an intent to suggest new directions for stress research.

Brief Review of Person–Environment Fit Theory and Findings

Theory

A number of theories of human stress (e.g., Pervin, 1968; French, Rodgers, and Cobb, 1974) and performance (McGrath, 1976) are based on the programmatic view that behaviour is a function of characteristics of the person and of the environment (Lewin, 1935; Murray, 1938). The model detailed briefly here is that proposed by French and his colleagues. The basic elements of the model are shown in Figure 1. The elaborations to be suggested are intended to build on the elements of this model and to be completely compatible with them.

Needs–supplies fit and abilities–demands fit. The theory distinguishes between two types of fit, each measured in terms of commensurate properties of the person and environment. There is the fit of needs and values of the person with the environmental supplies and opportunities to meet these needs and values. For example, people vary in their needs for achievement (e.g., Atkinson and Feather, 1966), and the environment varies in the extent to which it provides achievement-oriented situations (e.g., opportunities to attempt tasks where neither success nor failure are guaranteed). There is also the fit between the demands of the environment and the abilities of the person to meet those demands. For example, work environments vary in the amount of quantitative work load they impose, and employees vary in their ability to handle that work load.

Different points of view can influence whether PE fit is defined as needs–supplies misfit or demands–abilities misfit. The employee may choose to define fit in terms of occupational self-fulfilment; the employer may choose to define the employee's fit in terms of abilities to meet the environment's demands (the *employer's* needs). These distinctions can serve as a device for determining the exhaustiveness of any specific set of dimensions of PE fit even if the disctinction between the two types of fit does not necessarily represent two mutually exclusive categories. Harrison (1976) discusses the needs–supplies and abilities–demands distinction further, but it has received little study *per se*.[2]

Objective vs. subjective fit. A second element of the PE fit model is the distinction between the *objective* and *subjective* components of fit. In theory, one can measure P and E objectively (free of bias introduced by the person) as well as subjectively (inclusive of that bias). The correspondence between objective and subjective P is labelled 'accuracy of self-assessment' (self-awareness) whereas the correspondence between objective and subjective E is labelled 'contact with reality' (environmental awareness).

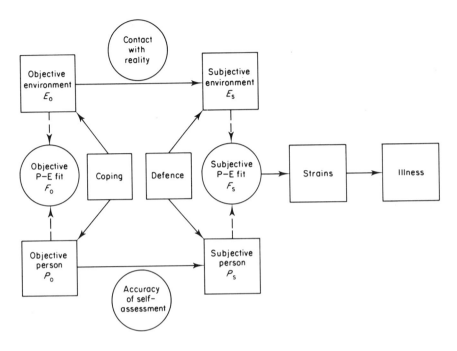

Figure 1   A model describing the effects of psychosocial stress in terms of fit between the person and the environment. Concepts within circles are discrepancies between the two adjoining concepts. Solid lines indicate causal effects. Broken lines indicate contributions to interaction effects (Harrison, 1978)

The objective measurement of both *P* and *E* remains a considerable challenge for the social sciences. Nevertheless, the conceptual distinction is one that is readily apparent in the applied fields of organizational development, clinical psychology, and counselling. Interventionists and counsellors deal with the client's abilities and inabilities to assess the self accurately (to know one's own needs and values, one's own limits) and to assess the environment accurately (to know the external resources for fostering or inhibiting need fulfilment, value expression, and role conformity or deviation).

'Accuracy of self-assessment' and 'contact with reality' are intended to be descriptive rather than prescriptive labels. Consequently, the reader should not assume that low strain and high mental health are necessarily associated with high degrees of either self- or environmental-knowledge. A little bit of distortion of reality can sometimes help a person face and overcome a stressor whereas an inability to distort the potential harm-producing nature of a stressor may render the person emotionally disabled (e.g., Lazarus, 1979).

PE fit theory recognizes processes of cognitive distortion as sources of discrepancies between objective and subjective components of fit. The environment itself also introduces distortions. For example, organizational and social networks serve as mechanisms for channelling, restricting, and modifying information accessible to the person (Katz and Kahn, 1978).

Figure 1 depicts subjective fit as more proximal than objective fit to psychological and physiological strain, and to health and illness. The ability to test this prediction fully awaits studies that assess both objective and subjective fit. Studies of commensurate objective and subjective stressors, such as studies of role conflict and work load (Kraut, 1965; French and Caplan, 1972; Frankenhauser, 1980) suggest that human perceptions of stressors do serve as intervening variables between objective stressors and the strains they produce.

Hypothesized relationships between fit and strain

Figure 2 illustrates three basic types of PE fit relationship. In a *U-shaped* relationship (curve A), excesses in the environment (such as too much work load), as well as deficits in the environment (such as too little work load), lead to higher levels of strain than the case where $P=E$. Excess elements of the environment may threaten one motive while deficits may threaten another. For example, too little work load may threaten the need for use of skills and abilities, whereas too much work load may threaten the need to achieve or to avoid failure.

In an *asymptotic* relationship (curve B), either an excess of P, but not a deficit, or an excess of E, but not a deficit, can lead to strain. For example, persons with a strong need for self-control (versus control by others or fate; e.g., Burger and Cooper, 1979) may feel threatened by too little opportunity for participation in decisions. Reducing this deficit will reduce the strain they experience. These same persons may experience little further reduction in strain once the opportunity for participation exceeds the minimum they find acceptable.

The third PE fit curve (curve C) represents the case where the absolute amount of one PE fit component (e.g., P), relative to the other (e.g., E) has a *linear* effect on strain. For example, in some work situations, the more work load one has *relative* to the amount one wants, the more strain. This is not the same as merely examining the amount of work load the person has *per se*, for in that case, *need* for work load is not considered. The methods for searching for these different curves is beyond the scope of this paper; a detailed description can be found elsewhere (Harrison, 1976; Caplan, Cobb, *et al.*, 1980).[3]

There are many other PE fit curves that represent modifications of the three forms just described (Kulka, 1979). For example, the U-shaped curve can be broadened at the base to represent the assumption that there is an interval of tolerance surrounding $P=E$, and that strain begins to increase only beyond the boundaries of that interval.

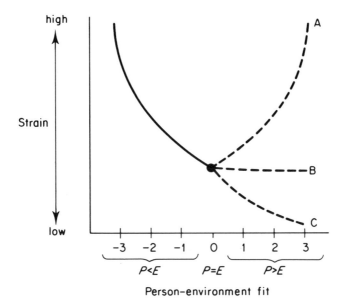

Figure 2 Three hypothetical shapes of the relationship between PE fit and strain. Curves B and C can also be drawn as their mirror images to depict functions which are their respective reverse opposites

One can also develop U-shaped curves that have their nadir at a point slightly beyond $P=E$. This type of curve has been observed in some analyses of PE fit in relationship to job satisfaction (e.g., Caplan, 1971). Such results may be due to measurement error, but they may also suggest that the most emotionally satisfying point of fit may be one that creates a bit of challenge (discomfort to be resolved).

If such data support the latter interpretation, the results may mitigate the sometimes-raised suggestion that subjective fit is merely a measure of satisfaction. If subjective fit were equivalent to emotional satisfaction, then the highest satisfaction should occur where $P=E$ and not at some other point. More importantly, from the perspective to PE fit theory, satisfaction and subjective fit are viewed as separate concepts — fit being a cognition, satisfaction being a positive affect.

Measurement of PE fit

Current methods of measuring subjective PE fit require the use of pairs of items. One member of the pair is a P item (need or ability) and the other member is an E item (environmental supply or demand). The P and E components are phrased with commensurate content (e.g., 'How much responsibility for persons do you have?' and 'How much would you like?'), and responses are obtained on 5 to 7 point scales (e.g., 1='None' and 5='A great deal').

The use of commensurate items distinguishes PE fit theory from other person–environment interactionist approaches (e.g., Bowers, 1973). In other approaches, *P* and *E* need not be assessed on commensurate dimensions. By using commensurately scaled measures of *P* and *E*, one can perform direct tests of hypotheses that deal with the nonlinear, interactive effects of discrepancies between *P* and *E* in terms of their original units of quantification. One may also assume that the more noncommensurate *P* is from *E*, the more irrelevant *P* and *E* will be in contributing to a state of PE misfit.

In studies of self-reported PE fit, an attempt is usually made to develop multi-item indices of fit in order to produce reasonably high coefficients of internal consistency (e.g., Caplan, *et al.*, 1980; French, Caplan, and Harrison, in press). There are a number of unresolved questions regarding just how these items should be phrased and regarding just how *P* and *E* should be combined. These questions will be reviewed briefly because they, like extensions of the theory, indicate new directions for stress research.

Scale contamination. Scales, such as the one given in the example above, involve relative judgements. The judgement of what is 'A great deal' of some demand in the environment forces the person to take into consideration some standard against which to judge that quantity. That standard may well be the person's own ability. For example, a moderate amount of assigned responsibility for the well-being of others, in an absolute sense, may be perceived of as quite *high* by a person who has a very low ability to assume such responsibility. The same absolute amount of responsibility may be perceived as *very little* responsibility by a person with a much higher capacity for assuming responsibility.

Consequently, the use of scales that elicit relative judgements increases the chances that *E* measures become contaminated with elements of *P* and vice versa. This may be one reason why it is not unusual to find *P* and *E* measures correlated ('r's ranged from .13 to .68 in a study of 23 different occupations; Caplan, *et al.*, 1980). Longitudinal designs will be necessary to determine the extent to which such correlation represents contamination and the extent to which the association represents some causal relationship (for example, persons with high needs for job complexity may seek out environments that provide such complexity).

The risk of contamination might be reduced considerably, but probably not completely, by the use of more concrete response scales. For example, one can assess 'number of hours you spend per day in an activity' and 'number of hours per day you *want* to spend in the activity', or 'number of patients you see per week' and 'number of patients you *want* to see per week', rather than 'how much work load do you have and want?'

Framing the stem. There is no adequate theory about when to assess PE fit with regard to needs–supplies fit and when with regard to abilities–demands fit. As an illustration, suppose one wanted to measure PE fit with regard to participation in decision making. If one was interested in needs–supplies fit, the E component might read 'how much *opportunity* is there to participate?' If one was interested in demands–abilities fit, the E measure might instead read 'how much (of the time) are you *required* to participate in decision making?' The difference between having 'an opportunity' to participate and being 'required' to do so is a nontrivial one. If one is interested in role demands of participation, one would emphasize the requirements of the role rather than the discretionary opportunities; otherwise the focus might be on 'opportunity'. If demands–ability misfit implies less self-control than needs–supplies misfit, items framed as demands–ability fit will yield the higher prediction of strain; otherwise needs–supplies framing may be advisable.

The measurement of the P component in particular raises further choices for the investigator. Does one assess preferences ('how much do you prefer?'), needs ('how much do you have to have?'), optimal or ideal desires ('how much would you want in the best of all possible circumstances?'), expectations based on perceived equity or perceived norms ('how much do you think you *should* get compared to other people with your skills and training?'), or minimally acceptable, satisficing (March and Simon, 1958) levels ('how little can you tolerate?')

In part, selection among alternatives such as these should be based on a theory that clearly specifies the alternative one wants (Wanous and Lawler, 1972). PE fit theory can probably tolerate most of these alternatives. Researchers of PE fit, however, have not systematically probed the theoretical and empirical consequences of these different framings.

Placement of items. Should each commensurate pair of P and E items be presented together? If so, which should come first, the P component or the E component? Should one ask all the P items and then ask all the E items (or the reverse)? If so grouped, should the P and E items appear near one another in the measurement instrument or be separated?

If one asks the P and E items in pairs, one runs the risk that the answer the person gives to the second member of the pair is biased by the response given to the first item. For example, respondents indicating that their job provides little supervisory responsibility may adopt a 'sour grapes' approach and indicate that the amount of responsibility that they want is also very little. If, however, one separates the P and E items from one another in the survey instrument, one may reduce consistency bias while increasing error because the respondent does not keep in mind the scaling used to answer one component when answering the other. So far no systematic research on the effects of ordering and formatting of PE fit questions has been conducted to resolve these issues.

Findings from PE fit theory

The first real test of a PE fit theory using commensurate measures of P and E appears to be the work by Pervin (1967a, 1967b). Dropping out of school for nonacademic reasons and school dissatisfaction were associated with a lack of fit between the amount of structuredness in the educational approach and the student's need for structure versus for academic autonomy.

The major tests of PE fit theory, as described here, have been conducted by Harrison and his colleagues (Harrison, 1976, 1978; Caplan, *et al.*, 1980; French, *et al* in press) on a sample of 23 different occupations; by Tannenbaum and Kuleck (1978) in 52 industrial plants in five countries; and by House (1972) on the community of Tecumseh. Tests of the theory have also been conducted by Kulka (1975), Kulka, Mann, and Klingcl (1980), and Kulka, Klingel, and Mann, (1980) on a sample of high-school students, and by Kahana, Liang, and Felton (1980) in a study of elderly persons. In these studies the relative power of PE fit to explain variance not already accounted for by P and E alone were explored via multivariate analyses (the Tannenbaum and Kuleck study does not analyse variance in this manner). Some of the findings have provided rather striking support for the theory. For example, Figures 3 and 4 show how PE fit, but not P or E, predicted depression in an occupationally stratified sample of 318 employees from 23 occupations (Caplan, *et al.*, 1980, pp. 90–91). In general, however, PE fit has explained only an additional 1% to 5% variance in strain. It has, however, consistently doubled the amount of variance explained.

Given the complexities of measurement and curve-fitting described earlier, the findings are encouraging. The percentage of variance that PE fit theory can explain in strain must be increased, however, if the theory is to deserve further attention in stress research. The next section on extensions of the theory suggests that beyond issues of measurement, the strength of findings so far may have been weak because the parameters of theory are not specified fully enough. Additions are suggested that might significantly increase the explanatory power of PE fit as a predictor of strain. The same issues of measurement that apply to the basic theory of PE fit also apply to the extensions that follow.

An Extension of PE Fit Theory

Current PE fit theory deals with dynamic concepts as well as the static ones reviewed so far. These dynamic concepts are defined here because they will

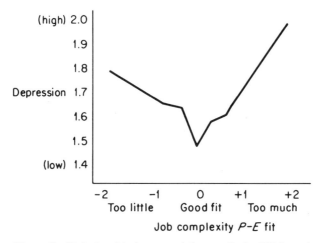

Figure 3   Relationship between job complexity PE fit and depression. Eta=0.26 ($p<.002$). N=318 men from 23 occupations. (From Caplan *et al.*, 1980, p. 91)

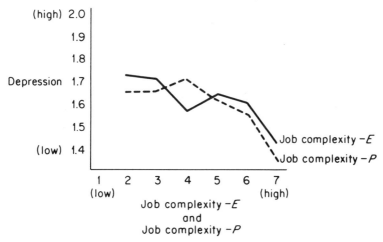

Figure 4   Relationships between scores on depression and scores on job complexity-E and job complexity-P. Etas=0.14 (NS) and 0.19 (NS) respectively. N=318 men from 23 occupations. (From Caplan *et al.*, 1980, p. 90)

be referred to in the elaborated model of PE fit. They are perhaps the most important and certainly the most neglected part of the theory in terms of research.

French, *et al.*, define the following adjustive techniques: (a) *coping* is a change in objective fit occurring either via a change in objective E_o, termed *environmental mastery*, or via a change in objective P_o, termed *adaptation*; (b) *defence* is a change in subjective PE fit occurring via changes in subjective E_s and subjective P_s *without* corresponding changes in objective fit.

French, *et al.*, make a number of deductions from the elements in Figure 1 which involve the dynamics of PE fit. These include the observation that a defensive *decrease* in E_s will decrease contact with reality when objective environmental supplies or demands exceed the amount of them perceived ($E_o > E_s$) but will increase contact with reality when the reverse is the case ($E_o < E_s$). Furthermore, a defensive *increase* in E_s will improve contact with reality when $E_o > E_s$ but will reduce contact with reality when $E_o < E_s$. Similar deductions can be made for the effects of defensive changes in P_s on accuracy of self-perception depending on the initial relations of P_o to P_s.

The elaborated PE fit model which follows includes the elements reviewed so far as well as components of fit that deal with the past and the present. These additional time perspectives are discussed in terms of how they give meaning to current levels of fit. They are also discussed in terms of how they help explain the nature of coping and particularly defense as those terms have been defined in the theory of PE fit of French, *et al.*

Figure 5 presents the elements of the model; it depicts fit as F and not as its components, P and E. The elaboration of F into P and E is deferred until after the elements of Figure 5 have been discussed.

Objective and subjective fit at three time points

As with the general model of PE fit described earlier, Figure 5 distinguishes between objective and subjective fit (F_o and F_s respectively). Each measure of fit is shown at a minimum of three time periods at which *measurement* occurs: $t-1$ indicates an objective past time period, $t0$ indicates the objective present time period, and $t1$ indicates an objective future time period.

The length of the intervals between periods of measurement is not specified in the model. The specification of the intervals is crucial when attempting to uncover causal relationships on the basis of hypothesized intervals of causation (such as Kenny, 1979). Furthermore, one must specify whether the vertical dashed lines in Figure 5 represent an objective interval of time into the past (or into the future) that is the same for every person or varies by individual, by culture (such as Levine, West, and Reis, 1980), or by other grouping. This important question for theory and measurement is not explored here.

Following Lewin (1951), perceived or subjective past, present, and future fit (F_s) are all assumed to exist in the objective present as time perspectives of the person. All these perspectives are hypothesized to influence the person's present behaviour.

The objective present (F_o) influences the person's behaviour only insofar

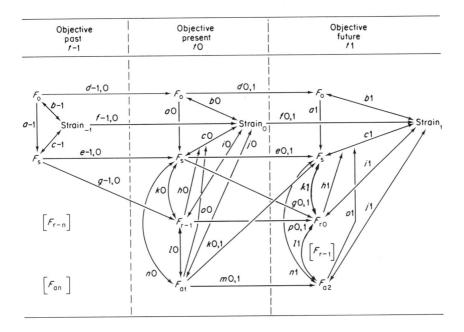

Figure 5 Past, present, and future fit (F). F_o, F_s, F_r, and F_a refer to objective, subjective, retrospected, and anticipated fit respectively. A numerical subscript refers to the wave of measurement about which the fit measure refers. Thus, F_{r-1} at $t0$ is a retrospection at $t0$ about $t–1$. The dashed vertical lines separate $t–1$, $t0$, and $t1$ from each other. Arrows between variables represent hypothesized causal paths. Arrows that intersect arrows represent conditioning or moderating effects. Letters on the arrows are used for reference in the text. Arrows with the same prefix represent the same relationship at different points or lags between times. The suffix denotes the time of measurement. If only one suffix number is listed (such as, $c–1$), the relationship occurs within one wave of data collection. If a second suffix number is listed (such as, $e–1,0$), the first number indicates the wave of measurement of the antecedent variable, and the second number indicates the wave of measurement of the consequent variable. F_{r-1}, and F_r and F_a at $t–1$, are in brackets to indicate that the effects are omitted for graphic simplicity. In a complete depiction of the model, the hypothesized effects of F_a and F_r on the other parameters in the model would be similar to those shown for F_a and F_r elsewhere in the model

as the person is aware of the elements of F_o or insofar as the elements have some unconscious impact on the behaviour of the person. For example, a warm fireplace in another room (objective environment) may influence the person's behaviour only to the extent that the person is aware of the fireplace or unconsciously benefits from the heat it puts out. If the other room is sealed off, so no heat reaches the person, or if the person does not know that by entering the other room one can derive additional warmth, the fireplace has no effect.

Perceptions and, where possible, objective measures, of the past, present, and future that were measured in the objective past (such as during a prior interview or period of observation) remain in the model as archived data for use by the scientific investigator. As will be discussed, these data from the past may predict to current and future perceptions of past, present, and future fit because they represent historical aspects of PE fit that may alter the person's store of knowledge about the self and about the environment. But the objectively archived past has no influence on the person's behaviour other than by the person's own awareness of its existence and its contents.

Arrows $a-1$, $a0$, and $a1$ (see Figure 5 for a description of the system for labelling these arrows) represent the hypothesis that subjective fit is determined by objective fit. Both objective and subjective misfit are hypothesized to have a statistically positive effect on strain in the past (arrows $b-1$ and $c-1$), present (arrows $b0$ and $c0$), and future periods (arrows $b1$ and $c1$).

In order to determine the extent to which current and future levels of misfit (both subjective and objective) have unique influences on strain, it is important to estimate and partial out the effects of antecedent levels of misfit and strain. The indirect effects of antecedent levels of misfit on strain in later time periods are derivable from the figure. For example, the effects of F_o at $t-1$ on strain at $t0$ can be derived as an expected link because F_o at $t-1$ influences F_o at $t0$ (arrow $d-1,0$), and strain at $t-1$ (arrow $b-1$). In turn, F_o at $t1$ and strain at $t-1$ influence strain at $t0$ (arrows $b0$ and $f-1,0$ respectively). The reader can trace other indirect paths and derive other relatively long links.

Strain, itself, contributes to its own subsequent levels over time (arrows $f-1,0$ and $f0,1$). Strain is hypothesized to make this contribution: (a) because some strains may have accumulative, sometimes long-term, sometimes irreversible effects; and (b) because some strains may act as causes of other strains. For example, atherosclerosis could be treated as irreversible in this model because there are no known *psychogenic* interventions which reduce the accumulation of arterial plaque. Furthermore, the production of atherosclerosis may eventually lead to angina pectoris and myocardial infarction, new strains. On the other hand, job dissatisfaction or depression may have reversible effects, although at high enough levels may lead to irreversible effects, such as suicide.

The stability of objective fit is represented by arrows with the prefix d. Thus, the stability of F_o from $t-1$ to $t0$ and from $t0$ to $t1$ are represented by $d-1,0$ and $d-0,1$. The stability of subjective fit is represented by arrows with the prefix e. The consistency of F_o and of F_s over time provide an indication of the *chronicity* versus *event-like* nature of the misfit. More is said about chronicity and event-like PE misfit in the detailed discussion of these elements that follows.

Retrospected fit

Up to this point, all of the elements discussed in Figure 5 are ones that appear in the original model of PE fit described earlier. Retrospections and anticipations of fit are now discussed as elements of an extended model of PE fit and strain.

Retrospected and anticipated fit have been given the notations F_r and F_a respectively in Figure 5. To indicate the period about which the person is asked to retrospect or anticipate, a modifier is added to the r and a to indicate the relevant time frame. For example, F_{r-1} indicates a retrospection about $t-1$, F_{r0} indicates retropsection about $t0$, and F_{a+1} indicates an anticipation of $t1$.

In theory, it is possible to obtain retrospections about a multitude of points in time. As an illustration, F_{r-1} at $t1$ is a retrospection about information from *two* waves ago at $t-1$. F_{r-1} at $t1$ has been put in brackets in Figure 5 to indicate that the linkages to and from it are intentionally omitted from the figure to simplify its graphics. The stability or repeat reliability of F_r is represented by arrow $p0,1$.

Along with the subjective fit (F_s), retrospected fit (F_r) is hypothesized to determine strain (arrow $i0$ at $t0$ and arrow $i1$ at $t1$). Retrospections are hypothesized to influence current strain because they evoke the vicarious experience of past fit or misfit. Retrospections are also hypothesized to have interactive effects with F_s on strain (the intersections of arrows $h0$ and $c0$ and or arrows $h1$ and $c1$). The nature of the interaction effect of F_r and F_s on strain is described in more detail below. For now it is noted that F_r is hypothesized to help the person determine whether the present level of fit is an improvement, worsening, or maintenance of the past level of PE fit.

The model includes the hypothesis that past subjective fit influences retrospections about that fit (arrows $g-1,0$ and $g0,1$). The relationship between subjective fit and the retrospection of it (arrows with the prefix g) can be labelled the *coefficient of recall*. The retrospections are subject to error, so that the relationship between them and past subjective fit is less than 1.00. Among the noted sources of error is the forgetting or underreporting of aspects of the past that reflect negatively on one's self concept (Cannell, Fisher, and Baker, 1965), that are not salient (Cannell, Miller, and Oksenberg, 1981), and that are generally negative or unpleasant (Holmes, 1970). Mood may also affect recall. Depressed persons, for example, may tend to recall more negative events than are recalled by nondepressed persons (e.g., Beck, 1976). This effect is discussed in more detail below.

Research suggests that with the passage of time, retrospections should represent the past as less under the person's control, less volitional *or* fortuitous, and more predetermined or inevitable (Janoff-Bulman and Brickman, 1982; Fischoff, 1975; Miller and Porter, 1980). This type of attribution bias is an important consideration in the extended model of PE fit when, as described below, goodness of fit is further differentiated into that which is *P*-produced or initiated and that which is *E*-produced or initiated.

Rather than being cause for dismay, these biasing influences on retrospections are of potential interest in the study of how PE fit affects strain. Such representations of the past may cause the person to either be pleased or dismayed with current fit, depending on whether retrospections by comparison, tint the past to be rosier ('the good old days' that never were) or worse than would be suggested by past PE fit panel data archived on the respondents.

Anticipated fit

Anticipations of future fit (F_a; arrows $j0$ and $j1$), like retrospections about past fit, are hypothesized to affect strain. The nature of these main effect relationships is discussed below, as are the hypothesized conditioning effects of anticipated fit (arrows $o0$ and $o1$) on the relationship between subjective fit and strain (arrows $c0$ and $c1$).

The association between anticipated fit and the resultant subjective fit (arrow $k0,1$) serves as an *index of subjective foresight*. This foresight refers to predicting *subjective* fit at the next wave. One can also deal with the foresight of anticipations with regard to *objective* fit at future time points. In studies of coping and adaptation, such an index can allow one to determine the extent to which the person had realistic expectations.

The assessment of anticipated fit, and objective and subjective fit about which the anticipation was elicited, allows one to make inferences about distortive influences on subjective fit. For example, consider the hypothesis that F_o influences F_s, although imperfectly. How might the measurement of anticipated fit help us identify the source of such imperfection? If we find that past anticipations of fit (e.g., arrow $k0,1$), rather than the resultant objective fit (e.g., arrow $a1$), predict F_s at $t1$ better, we will have identified a person for whom past expectations rather than current reality influences subjective perceptions of fit. Consequently, the defensive processes that reduce the agreement between F_0 and F_s can be identified partly in terms of distortions caused by past expectations.

Earlier it was noted that retrospection can be influenced by systematic biases. Are anticipations also subject to systematic biases? Research suggests that people's probability estimates of future events are influenced by: (a) the extent to which they know of similar events having already occurred (the availability heuristic suggested by Tversky and Kahneman, 1973); (b) the person's wishes about what should happen, particularly when the other available cues for making a prediction are very ambiguous (McGregor, 1938;

Cantril, 1938); and (c) the distance into the future about which the anticipation applies (Milburn, 1978). From a set of well-designed experiments,
Milburn determined that:

> negative events were seen as more likely than positive events but
> as decreasingly likely further in the future; conversely, positive
> events were predicted as increasingly likely over time, being seen
> as more likely than negative events at the final time period. (p. 17)

Consequently, F_a should be best ($P=E$) for long-term anticipations but
should be on the pessimistic side for short-term anticipations. It may be
advisable to examine both long- and short-term anticipations of PE fit in
order to determine their relative contributions to current levels of strain,
coping, and defence.

Relationships among retrospected, current subjective, and anticipated fit

The three forms of subjective fit all have double-headed arrows within each
objective time period in Figure 5. These arrows indicate that relationships
run both ways among these forms of fit. They may all simultaneously and
mutually influence one another (for example, the double-headed arrows $h0$,
$n0$, and $l0$). The linkages among these forms of subjective fit are hypothesized
to represent two basic processes: contrast effects and expectancies.

Contrast effects occur when the degree of fit in one of the three time frames
produces fit in another time frame so that the two forms of fit are negatively
correlated. These hypothesized effects involve a form of relative deprivation
(Merton and Kitt, 1950) in which there are comparisons across time (Brickman and Campbell, 1971, refer to these as temporal discrepancies, as distinguished from social comparisons).

For example, an employee may anticipate that the future will provide
better PE fit on responsibility for persons than the present. The person's
optimism about better resources to carry out responsibility in the future may
raise the person's aspirations for the present (P), and thereby lead to an
increase in PE misfit. Thus optimism might, paradoxically, lead to increased
feelings of dissatisfaction with the present. Similarly, pessimism about future
fit may lead to increased satisfaction with the present by lowering the person's
aspirations (P) with regard to the present. These dynamics are reminiscent
of the aphorism: 'Be happy with what you have. Things could be worse.'

Some contrast effects may be produced by the type of response judgements
we ask people to make regarding PE fit. Specifically, the more concrete the
response scale, the less likely that subjective past, present, and anticipated
fit will be correlated. For example, suppose we are assessing PE fit with
regard to 'How many pages can you type a day?' and 'How many are you

given to type a day?' We could choose either the concrete response scale 'give actual number of pages' or the abstract response scale 'none', 'a few', 'some', 'a lot', and 'an extreme amount'. If we choose the latter scale, ratings such as 'some' for any one time frame may be defined in terms of what was the most and the least amount of typing the person has had in some particular period of time. The period of time can easily include both the past as well as the anticipated future, and therefore these subjective time frames will tend to become intercorrelated. Concrete response scales should, accordingly, reduce such correlations among F_r, F_s, and F_a.

Some research suggests that temporal comparison (such as comparing present performance with past performance) rather than social comparison ('how am I doing relative to other people like myself?') is a better predictor of aspirations and expectations (Fishbein, Raven, and Hunter, 1963). It is possible, however, that both types of comparison processes may affect well-being and behaviour. For example, anticipated fit could be influenced by views of one's past fit as well as by comparisons with how well one thinks others will be doing in the future on the same dimension of PE fit. This area of PE fit research remains to be explored.

Expectancy effects may take on a variety of forms. These forms involve the parameters of (a) stability, (b) controllability, (c) forseeability, and (d) similarity (or generalizability; see Lewin, 1951). These elements have been discussed in another area of research dealing with expectations — learned helplessness (e.g., Abramson, Seligman, and Teasdale, 1978; Wortman and Dintzer, 1978).

If the person expects stability in *P and E* over time, then anticipated fit (F_a) is likely to be positively correlated with current subjective (F_s) and retrospected fit (F_r). On the other hand, if the person expects instability in *P or E*, then F_a is likely to be uncorrelated with F_s or F_r. Similarly, if either *P* or *E* are viewed as uncontrollable or unforseeable, then relationships between F_a and F_r or F_s are likely to be weak merely because anticipations of future fit may be subjectively unreliable.

Although stability may be a necessary condition for expecting that perceptions of fit in one time frame will predict perceptions of fit in a subsequent time frame, it is not a sufficient condition. For example, a person with a perceived history of helplessness (Seligman, 1975) may view an increase in current PE fit as a fluke, discount it, and still anticipate relatively high levels of future misfit. In such a case, current fit would be unrelated to anticipated fit because the person perceives of the world as *stably* uncontrollable. Similarly, a person with a history of past success may discount a current failure as a fluke and anticipate continued success in the future. As the future turns into the present, these histories of success and failure may be maintained or altered with attendant cognitive consequences for perceiving F_r, F_s, and F_a.

With regard to controllability, past expectations may not necessarily lead to anticipations of future controllability. If the person expects that the present will be more controllable than other time frames, either past or future, then F_r and F_a may be uncorrelated with present fit. Such expectations might motivate the person to create the illusion of control (Langer, 1975) in the present by creating a retrospection of a *past* period as having relatively less control. The amount of distortion to be introduced in supporting this illusion would be determined by the amount of control the person perceived currently. Alternatively, the same illusion of more control in the present could be created by retrospecting past control accurately while distorting current PE fit with regard to controllability. It is likely that distortion of the past to make it less self-controlled will be preferred to distortion of the present to make it more self-controlled. For one thing, such a preference is consistent with studies cited above that suggest that people tend to view the past as more predetermined and less volitional. Second, it may be easier to distort the past than the present because recollections may be less subject to consensual pressure from others (Asch, 1956) than are perceptions of the present. In any event, theory and research are required to determine the extent to which such illusions of control are produced by distortions of F_r, F_s, or F_a.

To the extent that subjective past, present, and anticipated fit are perceived to be similar in terms of the dimensions of fit they represent (holding constant stability, controllability, and forseeability), they will be positively correlated. As an example, F_s and F_a will be most strongly correlated when both deal with quantitative work load (such as number of deadlines faced). They will be less strongly correlated when F_s deals with general quantitative work load and F_r deals with a specific form of work load, responsibility for others. And they will be even less strongly related when F_s deals with quantitative work load and F_a deals with an orthogonal dimension, role ambiguity (how well defined are the tasks).

The consideration of contrast and expectancy effects raises more questions than answers for social science. We need theory and research to determine the relative contributions of contrast and expectancy effects in determining: (a) the relationships among perceived past, present, and future PE fit; and (b) the effects of these three time perspectives on current levels of strain and other response to misfit (such as coping). We need theory and research about the extent to which people will distort perceptions of one time frame and not another in order to support expectancies that they have about self (P) and environment (E). For example, will people distort to others the past or future more than the present because the social costs are less? This would be the case if the distorter reasons, for example, that others cannot as easily verify distortions of the past, whereas others can more easily observe the present and draw their own conclusions. Finally, we need theory and research on contrast effects to determine if optimism (or pessimism) about future fit increases current subjective misfit, then does the effect of anticipated PE fit on strain cancel out the effect of current fit on strain, or does the perception of current misfit have a stronger net effect?

Effects of strain on PE fit and vice versa

Figure 5 depicts hypothesized effects of PE fit on strain, and the reverse. These effects are shown as double arrows between measures of fit and strain within time frames ($t-1$, $t0$, $t1$). Arrows from strain at one point in time to fit at a subsequent point in time, like arrows from PE fit at one point in time to strain at a subsequent point, have been omitted from the figure; they are, nevertheless, derivable.

PE fit theory has been concerned primarily with the role of strain as an outcome of misfit. Nevertheless, strain may affect PE fit, and so, both directions of effect are discussed in the text. With regard to the effects of strain, they are hypothesized to be both direct (represented in Figure 5) and indirect (not represented in Figure 5).

Direct effects of strain. Strain may have effects on objective fit (F_o) by undermining the person's objective abilities to meet objective demands. For example, the classic Yerkes–Dodson curve relating anxiety and performance suggests that excessive as well as inadequate amounts of anxiety may create misfit between the person's abilities and the demands of a test.

Strain may have effects on subjective fit (F_s) by directly altering the person's subjective perceptions of abilities. Depressed persons, for example, tend to have low self-esteem (e.g., Peterson, Schwartz, and Seligman, 1981).

Indirect effects of strain. Strain may produce a filter between objective fit and its perception. For example, depressed persons may have characterological expectancies of low ability (Janoff-Bulman, 1979) and of an environment which is uncontrollable or noncontingent upon their behaviour (Seligman, 1975). They may be overly sensitive to objective information that confirms such expectancies and overly insensitive to information that disconfirms such expectancies (e.g., Beck, 1976).

Knowing the affective state of the person may also help one infer relationships among subjective retrospected, present, and anticipated PE fit. Persons experiencing anxiety may view the future as uncertain and ambiguous (and the ambiguity as undesirable; Archer, 1979). Consequently their anticipations of future fit should be uncorrelated with subjective retrospected or current fit because their anticipations tend to be unreliable and uncertain. Depressed persons may have stable expectations of poor PE fit (Arieti, 1970), and this stability should contribute to associations between subjective retrospected, current, and anticipated fit.

Acute events versus chronic stressors

In describing the model in Figure 5, brief reference has been made to indicators of each elements' stabilities over time. Stability is now discussed in terms of *chronic conditions* versus *acute events*. These two descriptors have, to some extent, represented a regrettable division of focus in stress research on either life events or chronic stressors. It seems more desirable to view acute and chronic as opposite ends of a gradient of change over time.

The continuum is important because one may decide to weight the strain-producing effects of event-like acute onsets of stressors as different from chronic events. For example, one could assume that some acute events are potentially less predictable and consequently it is more difficult to prepare for them via rehearsal and other strategies of anticipation (Janis, 1962). Or one might assume that acute events use up more adaptive resources of the person, lacking the inertia of steady-state chronic conditions. Chronic events, on the other hand, may produce both long-term accumulating effects as well as adaptation.

Applying these weighting strategies requires a theory that specifies the extent to which the ups and downs of stressors are more (or less) harmful than an evenness of high levels of stressors. Glass (1977), for example, proposes such a theory to explain the high risk of coronary heart disease among Type A persons. The theory hypothesizes that the reactivity of Type A persons to uncontrollable, intermittent events, produces lability in certain biochemicals, and variability in these biochemicals promotes atherosclerosis.

From Figure 5 one can derive at least *eight* types of indices of the degree of chronicity of stressors:

(a) The comparison of F_o over time by the investigator determines the *objective chronicity* of a stressor.

(b) The comparison of F_s over time determines the extent to which subjective stressors have been chronic or event-like. This can be termed *derived subjective chronicity*.

(c) The comparison of F_r about several past points of time and current F_s will allow the investigator to infer the extent to which a stressor is perceived by the respondent as chronic or acute. This can be called *inferred* (or more properly, *investigator-inferred*) *subjective chronicity*.

(d) The person's direct judgement of the chronicity or event-like nature of the stressor (e.g., 1 = has been continuous for the last 24 months, 2 = has been intermittent over the last 24 months, 3 = has occurred only once in the last 24 months, and so on) ignores measurement of F_s, F_r, and F_o and can be called *directly reported subjective chronicity*.

(e) One can also deal with anticipations of future chronicity. In doing so, one would distinguish between past and future chronicity. For example, some events might be chronic in the past and anticipated future.

Some events may have an acute onset (the person is told 'you have high blood pressure') and is told to expect the condition to be chronic ('it usually requires treatment for the rest of one's life.') One can derive *anticipated objective chronicity* (e.g., the physician's diagnosis of the disease as chronic or acute) and the three measures of subjective chronicity described above, but with regard to the anticipated future: *anticipated derived subjective chronicity, anticipated investigator-inferred subjective chronicity*, and *anticipated directly reported subjective chronicity*.

By comparing these different concepts and related modes of assessing chronicity, one can make deductions about the dynamics of adjustment. For example, a person may feel overloaded today (F_s at $t0$) and may believe that this condition did *not* exist at $t-1$ (F_{r-1}). We may find out, from the archived $t-1$ interview, however, that the person *did* feel overloaded then. Consequently, the person has been, in terms of *derived subjective chronicity*, under chronic overload, but psychologically is denying (repressing) that this was the case. Accordingly, one might hypothesize that denial will keep the person from taking steps to reduce the misfit if the person erringly perceives misfit to be transitory. While the chronic nature of such a person's subjective misfit continues to generate strain, the subjective denial of its chronicity ('it is only a passing thing') continues to maintain the person's exposure to an unchanging, potentially unhealthy situation. Realization by the person that overload existed at $t-1$, too, may lead the person to take some steps to either modify self, situation, or both. If the person cannot leave the situation, then denial may be a useful defensive strategy for avoiding feelings of helplessness and depression.

Improved prediction of strain: F_r and F_a modify predictions of strain based only on F_s

Improved prediction of strain by jointly considering present and past fit. Table 1 presents some hypothetical data on nine persons, A through I. Assume that the data deal with fit on role ambiguity in a work situation, and that the persons with PE fit scores greater than zero have a greater need for role clarity than can be met by the formal guidelines and communicated expectations of others in the organization. Then the data in the fourth column of Table 1 (present fit) indicate that three persons have misfit scores of $+2$, three persons have scores of $+1$, and three persons have perfect fit scores of 0. This is usually all the information one has about PE fit in most studies.

To keep matters simple, let us assume that only a rank-ordering of PE fit and strain data is justified in looking at their relationship, and that the relationship between PE misfit and strain is positive. Then, persons A

Table 1   Hypothetical fit scores in retrospected past and present time frames

Person	Subjective PE fit				
	Past $(t-2)$	Past $(t-1)$	Present $(t0)$	Change $(t-1$ vs. $t0)$	Inferred subjective chronicity
A	+2	+4	+2	improved (−2)	low
B	+2	+2	+2	stable (0)	high
C	0	0	+2	worsened (+2)	medium
D	+4	+4	+1	improved (−3)	medium
E	+1	+2	+1	improved (−1)	low
F	+1	0	+1	worsened (+1)	low
G	0	+4	0	improved (−4)	low
H	+2	+2	0	improved (−2)	medium
I	0	0	0	stable (0)	high

Note: + score indicates $(P>E)$, 0 indicates $(P=E)$

through C would be ranked has having the highest level of strain (median rank of 2), persons D, E, F would have an intermediate level (median rank of 5), and persons G through I would have a median rank of 8. These ranks have been entered in Table 2 for later reference.

Now suppose we are given some additional information about each of these nine persons. The additional information consists of their retrospections of past PE fit at $t-1$ (F_{r-1}) assessed on the same dimensions as present fit. As shown in Table 1, persons A through C have F_r scores of +4, +2, and 0 respectively. With this additional information, one can develop a differentiated picture about how the +2s that persons A through C have in common for present PE fit differ in meaning among these three persons. For person A, the current +2 represents an improvement in perceived fit. For person B, the current +2 represents a maintenance of a prior state. For person C, the current +2 represents a worsening of fit compared with the perceived past.

Likewise, for persons D through F note that information about their past perceived fit allows one to make differentiations regarding meaning of the current fit scores that they have in common. The same can be said for persons G, H, and I.

Using the information about F_{r-1}, assume that the change from past to present fit influences strain (essentially the additive influence of both past and current fit in a multiple regression model).[4] Further assume that any change which represents improvement in fit reduces strain and that any change which represents a worsening in fit increases strain. Then the ranking of persons A through H changes from the ordering which would have been based solely on knowing only their scores on present PE fit to an ordering like that shown in column (b) of Table 2. The resultant prediction of who has the highest and lowest levels of strain is markedly different from the one in the column for present PE fit in Table 2.

Table 2   Rank ordering of persons A through I based on present fit, change from past to present fit, and anticipated change from present to future

	Rank ordering assuming strain is positively influenced by:						
	(a) Present fit only		(b) Change from past to present fit		(c) Anticipated change from present to future		(d) Median of past, present, anticipated
Strain	Person	rank	Person	rank	Person	rank	Person	rank
high			C	1	D	1		
↑	A,B,C	2	F	2			C	2
					C,I	2.5		
			B,I	3.5			B,I	3.5
					G	4		
	D,E,F	5	E	5			D,E,F	5
					B,H	5.5		
			A,H	6.5			A,H	6.5
					E,F	7.5		
↓	G,H,I	8	D	8			G	8
low			G	9	A	9		

Note: Table entries derived from Tables 1 and 3

Now consider some additional information about the nine hypothetical cases in Table 1 — the retrospection of two measurement periods ago (F_{t-2}). These data are presented in the second column of Table 1. With this additional information one can judge (a) the extent to which PE fit (misfit) is chronic, and (b) if chronic, whether the degree of fit is chronically low or high.

The final column of Table 1 indicates the new characterizations of the PE fit stressor that are now possible. Although persons A through C all have the same present subjective PE fit score, A's score is part of low inferred chronicity, B's is part of medium chronicity, and C's is part of high chronicity. Similar distinctions can be made for persons D through F and G through I. Taking into account the amount of chronicity, one can modify the predictions of strain for these persons to reflect either more strain for chronic, high stressors than for acute, high stressors; or the reverse, depending on one's specific hypothesis about the role of episodic and chronic stressors, and retrospections of them, on well-being.

Improved prediction of strain by jointly considering current fit and future fit. Table 3 presents the hypothetical data from persons A through I in Table 1, but now includes anticipated fit scores (F_a). This additional information alters further the predictions of strain from what they would be if they were based on only current levels of fit. Although persons A through C all have the same current fit score, +2, their anticipations vary. Person A anticipates some improvement, person B anticipates a stable situation, and person C antici- pates things getting worse. Similar distinctions regarding anticipated fit can be made for the other two groups of persons whose within-group current fit scores are the same, persons D through F and G through I.

If one were to hypothesize that the greater the anticipated improvement, the greater the reduction in strain, then one might rank persons A through

Table 3 Hypothetical fit scores in the past, present, and anticipated future time frames

Person	PE fit			Derived expected change from current to anticipated	Related to past to present trend?
	Retrospected past (F_{r-1})	Present (F_{s0})	Anticipated (F_{a+1})		
A	+4	+2	0	improved (−2)	yes
B	+2	+2	+2	stable (0)	yes
C	0	+2	+4	worse (+2)	yes
D	+4	+1	+4	worse (+3)	no
E	+2	+1	0	improved (−1)	yes
F	0	+1	0	improved (−1)	no
G	+4	0	+1	worse (+1)	no
H	+2	0	−2	worse (−2)	yes
I	0	0	+2	worse (+2)	no

Note: + scores indicate ($P>E$), 0 scores ($P=E$), and − scores ($P<E$)

I in the order represented in column (c), in Table 2. This ranking is unrelated linearly to the predictions of the rankings on strain that were made knowing only the present levels of PE fit (column (a)) or the change from past to present levels (column (b)).

Table 2 shows that there are now three separate rankings of the nine respondents based on changes from past to present fit, and one based on anticipations in relation to current fit. What is the combined effect of each of these hypotheses operating simultaneously?

There are many opportunities here for testing competing theories of how past, present, and anticipated fit combine to affect strain. For example, one model might weight the present state of fit as more important than the effect of the past and anticipated future. Another model might modify the above scheme by weighting the effect of future as more important than the past. One may wish to weight personally undesirable changes, accomplished or anticipated (e.g., Ross and Mirowsky, 1979), as stronger predictors of strain than personally desirable changes. Still other models might build in concepts that allow for individual differences in weighting schemes (for example, some people may focus on the future, others may focus on the present, and still others may live in the past). Some models may provide different weighting schemes depending on the dependent variables. For example, anxiety might be characterized by higher weighting of the unpleasant future, satisfaction–dissatisfaction might be more influenced by current conditions, and grief might be focused on the past.

To illustrate a combined effect of past, present, and anticipated fit, an example will be presented that assumes equal weighting of present fit and of the effects of change from past to current and current to anticipated fit. Given that the data are ordinal, we will settle for taking the median rank on strain of the ranks assigned for the effects of current fit (column (a)), past to current fit (column (b)), and current to anticipated fit (column (c)) for each person. For example, for person A, the median would be 6.5 (based on the ranks 2, 6.5, and 9 in columns (a), (b), and (c) respectively). These resulting ranks appear in Table 2, column (d). The resulting rank-ordering of persons A through I shows little linear relationship to their ranks on present fit (column (a)) or to the two other rankings in Table 2. This relatively naïve exercise with hypothetical data should be sufficient to suggest that if past and anticipated fit influence strain, then attempts to predict a person's level of strain knowing only current levels of misfit could involve considerable error.

Specifying *P* and *E* in Past, Present, and Future Fit

So far, the discussion of the elaborated model of PE fit has dealt only with *F*. Now the discussion broadens to consider *P* and *E* as separate components of *F*. By considering *P* and *E*, a number of deductions and hypotheses are generated.

Table 4 presents nine more hypothetical cases in order to illustrate the roles of *P* and *E* in a model of past, present, and anticipated fit. For the moment, assume that the data in Table 4 deal with objective fit and with the objective components of fit, P_o and E_o for the past ($t-1$), present ($t0$) and a future time frame ($t1$) that we will assume was measured eventually.

Table 4 Hypothetical past, present, and future fit scores in terms of *P* and *E*

Person	$t-1$			$t0$			$t1$			Trend
	P	*E*	*F*	*P*	*E*	*F*	*P*	*E*	*F*	
Q	5	1	+4	5	3	+2	5	5	0	improvement via *E* (mastery, change of venue)
R	5	1	+4	3	1	+2	1	1	0	improvement via change in *P* (needs)
S	5	1	+4	4	2	+2	3	3	0	improvement via compromise (*P* and *E*)
T	5	5	0	5	3	+2	5	1	+4	worsening via change in *E* without change in *P*
U	1	1	0	3	1	+2	5	1	+4	worsening via change in *P* without change in *E*
V	3	3	0	4	2	+2	5	1	+4	worsening via change in *P* and in *E*
W	3	3	0	3	3	0	3	3	0	stabilized, *P* and *E* stable
X	3	3	0	2	2	0	3	3	0	stabilized, *P* and *E* covary
Y	5	1	+4	1	4	−3	4	2	+2	'Closing' pattern

Equifinal varieties of change in fit

The data in Table 4 show, in part, the property of equifinality — there is more than one way to arrive at the same state of PE fit. The ways represent strategies as well as combinations of coincident forces in *P* and *E*.

Ways to improve fit. Persons Q, R, and S in Table 4 all have the same trend over the three time periods shown, an improvement from $F = +4$ (unmet need for role clarity, for example) at $t-1$, to $F = 0$ (perfect fit on role clarity) at $t1$. An inspection of the *P* and *E* components for these three persons shows, however, that they have each achieved this improvement in their own way. Person Q has done so via an increase in *E* to meet his needs (for example, perhaps person Q obtained from a supervisor a better clarification of how the job was supposed to be carried out). No change in *E* has occurred for person R; instead, R's need for role clarity has abated some (perhaps alienation or apathy have taken their toll). Finally, in the case of person S, some compromise has occurred. Need for clarity went down a bit and amount of role information went up a bit. Some other details of these three first cases will be discussed below after examining the other varieties of changes over time in PE fit.

Person Y represents a *closing pattern*, as in gunnery. The fit score hovers around 0, getting closer in *absolute* distance from it by moving from 4 to −3 to 2. It is not clear from such data whether person Y is changing aspirations to meet E's supplies of them or whether E (the supervisor, for example) is trying to meet person Y's needs by altering the supplies — each actor responding with a time lag of 1. Perhaps the supervisor is attempting to fulfil person Y's needs, if Y would just keep them constant long enough for the supervisor to do so. One needs to distinguish between P-initiated and E-initiated change in order to determine who is adjusting to whom. This topic will be discussed in more detail shortly.

Ways to worsen fit. To continue with Table 4, persons T, U, and V represent cases of worsening over time rather than improving. All three show movement in their fit scores from 0 to 2 to 4 across time, yet like Q, R, and S, each case represents a different dynamic of adjusting (maladjusting, to be correct). Person T, like person Q, maintains P while E gets worse rather than better (need for information stays the same but amount of information decreases).

For person U, fit worsens because E stays constant while P (need for information) grows. Consider, for example, the employee who is given an introductory briefing the first day on the job and for whom it is assumed that no other information is needed. The employee likewise cannot think of any questions the first day ($P=E$). But as the employee becomes more and more acquainted with the details of the role, the need for more information increases ($P>E$). Or to take another example, a rumour about employee lay-offs circulates but the company remains hushed on its plans (so P regarding need for information is slightly greater than E regarding supply of information). Formal channels of information show little increase while employee needs for information skyrocket (P regarding need for information becomes much greater than E regarding supply of information).

Person V is an example of 'reverse compromise'. Both the supplies in the environment and the needs of the person grow apart from one another.

Ways of maintaining stability. Two of the remaining cases in Table 4, persons W and X, represent *stabilized patterns*. For persons W and X, fit is maintained over time. For person W, however, the levels of P and E remain *invariant* whereas for person X the levels of fit *covary* (3,3; 2,2; 3,3). In the example of person X, we have someone who stays adjusted by changing P to meet E or vice versa. Again the PE fit scores by themselves do not necessarily give us information about *who* (P or E) changed P or E. The potential importance of such information in a model of stress and well-being is discussed next.

E-initiated versus P-initiated changes in E and in P

Although the cases in Table 4 are plausible examples of the adjustive process, they contain some ambiguities. In the example of person Q, for example, we do not know if E increased because: (a) person Q initiated a request for more information (environmental mastery); (b) more information was coming because E (the supervisor) decided there was a need; or (c) some combination of these two processes. This example points up the need to specify the extent to which changes in *E* are P-initiated, E-initiated, or both.[5]

Similarly, we need to be able to specify the extent to which changes in *P* are P-initiated or E-initiated. For example, a potential lowering of aspirations, such as the case of person R, could be the result of inputs by others ('don't get your hopes up; in this organization you're lucky to know when the lunch whistle blows'), or could be the result of cognitions by P that P's needs (or abilities) should be changed.

Hypotheses about effects of P-*initiated versus* E-*initiated change in* PE *fit*

The definition of certain terms is important in the hypotheses that follow. E-initiated subjective fit and misfit will refer primarily to cases where E stands for other persons or groups. Other E-initiated changes could be those due to impersonal elements such as chance, illness, or general aspects of the environment such as the economic climate. The latter are probably important influences on well-being. Nevertheless, the discussion makes no attempt to deal with these other aspects of E-initiated changes in *P* or *E* nor to consider how they have similar or different effects than E-initiated changes in *P* or *E* that are produced by persons.

P-initiated change in *P* or *E* will refer only to cases where the person does not feel compelled by some powerful other (E) to initiate change. In cases of such coercion, it is assumed that the hypothesized effects of P-initiated change in fit or misfit would be akin to that of an E-initiated change. Stated as a hypothesis, the more a P-initiated change is the result of perceived influence from E, the more likely the effect of the P-initiated change will be similar to an effect which is E-initiated. Similarly, to the extent that the person perceives that an E-initiated change ('my work group stood up for me and got the boss off my back') is P-initiated ('the work group did it only because I reminded them of our pledge to stick together'), the hypothesized effects will be similar to a P-initiated change. Clarifying such issues should be a matter of good specification in both measurement and theory.

The term 'toleration' is used in the following hypotheses specifically to refer to: (a) the amount of subjective misfit the person will withstand before attempting to reduce the misfit, multiplied by (b) the amount of time the person will spend in a perceived misfit situation before attempting to alter the perceived misfit. One can also define toleration in terms of the ability to withstand objective levels of misfit. It is usually this definition which is used in laboratory experiments in which stressors are manipulated objectively and assumed to be perceived as manipulated.

Increases in subjective misfit will lead to lower levels of strain if they are perceived as P-initiated rather than E-initiated. Furthermore, increases in subjective misfit will be tolerated more if they are perceived as P-initiated rather than E-initiated.

The rationale for these hypotheses comes from the literature on control and distress (see the review by Thompson, 1981). Some studies show that personal control helps people tolerate stressors better (stay in the situation longer) although their strain may not be reduced (e.g., Mills and Krantz, 1979, Experiment 2). Other studies show that personal control reduces strain (e.g., Langer and Rodin, 1976; Houston, 1977).

Thompson (1981) describes three theories regarding how controllable stressors may affect tolerance of stressors (stay in the situation longer) and of strain (withstand more discomfort). One theory is that control (or perceived control, or perceptions that the change is P-initiated) *gives people predictability*, lessening cognitive overload (e.g., Seligman, Maier, and Solomon, 1971). A second theory states that controllability *satisfies needs for a sense of mastery* (deCharms, 1968). A third theory is that having control provides the *assurance that one will not face an event that is beyond the limits of one's endurance*. This means that one is assured that one will be able to minimize maximum future danger (Miller, 1979; Lefcourt, 1973; Lazarus, 1966). Of these three theories, the last two seem particularly supportive of the proposition that subjective misfit, if P-initiated, is less likely to produce strain and is more tolerable.

Following the second theory, even if P-initiated behaviour leads to increased misfit in one domain (for example, refusing charity even if the refusal prevents one from fulfilling certain material needs), it may still be preferred by the person if it satisfies what the person believes is a stronger need — the need to be independent of others and symbolically in control of one's life (for better or worse; see also Thompson, 1981, p. 98). In such a case, satisfying the need to be independent should reduce the strain of guilt about having unfulfillable obligations to others. It may have little effect, however, on another strain — anxiety about being able to meet one's needs for material resources.

Following the third theory, P-initiated changes in E_o and in P_o provide the person with the reassurance that the rate of change and amount of change are under personal control. This cognition is assumed to be anxiety-reducing, particularly when the person (a) believes that the change can be harmful if not handled properly, and (b) does not trust others to be able to sense when harm has occurred. Following French and Raven's (1959) theory of social power, more tolerance of misfit and less strain, particularly anxiety, might be generated where the basis of power for E-initiated misfit is referent or expert than where the basis of power is coercive or legitimate. The latter bases of power, of course, threaten the need for choice because they preclude it by definition.

The above PE fit hypotheses state that it is better, in terms of tolerance of stressors and resultant strain, to bring misfit upon oneself than to have someone else produce one's misfit. The next hypothesis states that experiencing *fit* is also better if one sees the fit as self- rather than other-produced. *Increases in subjective fit will lead to greater reductions in strain if they are perceived as P-initiated rather than E-initiated.* The rationale for this hypothesis is that the attainment of fit, while producing reductions in strain via direct effects on reduced misfit, produces additional positive affect deriving from the *joy of problem resolution* or of mastery (deCharms, 1968; Jahoda, 1958). This hypothesis assumes that the act of resolving misfit is inherently pleasurable. It is hypothesized to be even more pleasurable for persons high on need for control (e.g., Burger and Cooper, 1979).

This hypothesis derives in part from the theory of reactance (Brehm, 1966). Increasing PE fit against the will of the person is hypothesized to threaten needs for personal control and to lead to attempts to restore prior levels of misfit in order to restore personal control.

Although P-initiated change in subjective fit is hypothesized to reduce strain more than E-initiated change, not all changes in fit which are P-initiated are expected to be equally strain-reducing. For example, P-initiated change in subjective fit which is accomplished by a lowering of aspirations (lowering of *P*) may be accompanied by a sense of failure, disappointment, and depression. On the other hand, PE fit theory would predict that if the lowering of aspirations results in better PE fit, there should also be a decrease in negative affect. If both these hypotheses are confirmed, then one would need to determine if there is some sequence of these conflicting affects, and if there are cancelling effects of negative and positive affect.

Persons attribute a change in fit to being either P-initiated or E-initiated depending on their expectations about personal controllability of the PE fit outcome. For example, persons with high self-esteem and high expectancies of personal control (personal responsibility) over their lives may view an increase in PE *misfit* as P-initiated. As a result, they may suffer more depression than persons with similar increases in misfit who have very low self-esteem (Feather and Davenport, 1981).

A full integration of attribution theory (e.g., Nisbett and Ross, 1980; Harvey, Ickes, and Kidd, 1976) with the model of PE fit presented here is not possible in this chapter.[6] Research on how P and E attributions are formed should allow one to predict when perceived changes in PE fit will be attributed to either P or E. One can examine the extent to which the person gave attributions for the change which were in keeping with the responsibility assigned for such changes by others who form the normative environment to which the person belongs. One can then examine the consequences for well-being of holding attributions that are or are not in line with the normative view.

P and E components of retrospected fit (F_r)

A comparison of retrospections of fit and subjective measures of fit from the period about which the retrospection deals can uncover the extent to which bias in recollection is due to changes in subjective E, subjective P or both. Persons may tend to forget that past demands were different from current ones, thus retrospecting an E similar to the E of today. They may forget that their abilities in the past were worse (or better) than they really were.

These errors of retrospection in P and E may be influenced by current levels of self-esteem and expectations of personal control (versus control by others or by chance). For example, persons with new-found low current self-esteem may generalize to their retrospections of the past: (a) downgrading the value of past achievements, and (b) overly attributing success to luck or to the aid of others and failure to a stable inability to master the environment. Persons with new-found high self-esteem may generalize to their retrospections of the past: (a) upgrading the value of past achievements, and (b) overly attributing success to internal control and failure to a lack of adequate effort (a transitory, volitional internal attribution). From the literature reviewed earlier on attributions, one would further expect that retrospections, in general, will represent past levels of fit as less under the person's control (less P-initiated) and more inevitable or predetermined (Janoff-Bulman and Brickman, 1982; Fischoff, 1975; Miller and Porter, 1980).

Selective errors of retrospection can lead to strain in cases where one would not predict strain on the basis of objective PE fit data about the past and present. People attempting to overcome a stressor may feel that they are not making progress, when in fact they are. The distance from the goal may seem unchanged despite the fact that their aspirations may be continually increasing as they attain higher levels of achievement (Lewin, *et al.*, 1944). For example, stroke patients on rehabilitative regimens may become discouraged because they cannot write clearly after a month. They may, however, fail to realize that one month ago they could not even hold a pencil. In terms of PE fit, these stroke patients may perceive that current and past fit (F_s and F_{r-1}) are both -1 (too little ability to meet expectations or demands) and that both cases of misfit are because $P = 3$ and $E = 4$. Subjectively to such patients, no progress has been made. It may be the case, however, that past subjective fit (F_{s-1}), although being -1, was the result of levels of ability and of expectations or demands that were both a point lower: $P = 2$ and $E = 3$. So the patients fail to note their progress in abilities and the rising expectations of others. Thus, we have an example where there are yoked increases in P and E without any change in the level of misfit.

The basic curves of PE fit theory in Figure 2 all show conditions under which an increase in PE misfit is hypothesized to produce an increase in strain. The example of yoked increases in P and E just described is of particular interest because it describes an effect of PE fit that is clearly *not* represented by the curves in Figure 2. The yoked increases are a case where strain increases *because* PE fit is static, that is, because subjective progress in reducing misfit is not being made (e.g., Abramson, Seligman, and Teasdale, 1978). This leads to the hypothesis that *lack of change in subjective misfit will increase strain if it threatens a person's need to achieve.* Persons with a low need to achieve would be less likely to show strain if misfit existed and did not change. Compared to persons high on need to achieve, they would remain in a static misfit situation longer without taking any steps to improve PE fit.

A second hypothesis is that the above effect will not occur even when need to achieve is high if the following conditions are met. Specifically, *a lack of change in subjective misfit will not increase strain, and may even be associated with a reduction in strain, if the person perceives that the lack of change is due to increases in abilities (P) accompanied by parallel increases in demands or expectations by others (E).* If someone can get the person to retrospect the P and E components of past fit more accurately, or in enough detail to realize that P (ability) has been increasing even though E (demands) have increased too, the person's sense of accomplishment should be enhanced and the need to achieve more closely met. These last two hypotheses suggest that the degree of subjective misfit may not be a sufficient determinant of strain; the perception that misfit does not change and the perception of *why* the misfit does not change may also be important.

PE fit on one dimension will be tolerated to the extent that its resolution would threaten PE fit on a more salient dimension. One *general* hypothesis in PE fit theory is that the resultant strain is a function of subjective PE fit across the array of dimensions of which the person is aware (for empirical support of this hypothesis, see Harrison, 1976, and French, *et al.*, in press). The above hypothesis regarding the relative salience of dimensions also follows from this general hypothesis.

As a specific example, suppose an employee is faced with the need to make a decision. Decision-making is part of this employee's task. The employee lacks adequate information (poor PE fit regarding demands versus abilities to make decisions). Assume that the immediate superior holds the necessary information. The employee will seek the information from the immediate superior only if the cost of doing so in terms of embarrassment and perceived lowered public self-esteem (Sherwood, 1965) is not greater than the cost of maintaining PE misfit regarding ability to make the decision. If, however, the cost of perceived loss of esteem from the superior is too high, information misfit will be tolerated. This toleration may manifest itself as vascillation or as being frozen into inaction, as might be present in a double-avoidance conflict (Brown, 1948).

The same example introduces a related corollary hypothesis. Specifically, *if the person does produce a change in* E *that increases PE fit* (such as seeking and obtaining information from the immediate superior), *the resultant strain will be lower to the extent that the change in* E *is attributed to the role obligation* (Rommetveit, 1954) *of another (E) rather than to the incompetence of the person (P).* This hypothesis should hold regardless of whether the person perceives the change to be P-initiated or E-initiated. Thus, the employee, having sought and received information from the immediate superior, will feel less embarrassed and more satisfied if the employee perceives that the superior gave the information because that is the superior's job rather than because the employee is incompetent in terms of the expected role. This hypothesis assumes that benefits of improved PE fit accrue most when they cost little (when they involve little loss of self-esteem, for example).

P and E components of anticipated fit (F_a)

What determines whether persons form F_a in terms of expectations that P will change or that E will change? At least part of the answer may lie in who the person sees as responsible for producing adjustment. Brickman and his colleagues (Brickman, *et al.*, 1982) provide a theory of four models of attribution of responsibility for problems and for their resolution that may be helpful in generating specific hypotheses about how anticipated fit will differ from current fit in terms of the components P_s and E_s.

In one model the person is not held responsible either for the source of misfit nor its solution (this is termed the 'medical model' because it describes the usual case of the hospitalized patient). Persons who hold this model will view future fit, like past misfit, to be the result of E-initiated forces or forces of circumstance.

In a second model, the person is held responsible for the problem but not for its solution (such as, Alcoholics Anonymous; this is termed the 'enlightenment model' by Brickman and his colleagues.) Persons who hold this model will view future fit as a matter of E-initiated forces or circumstance even though they view past levels of fit as P-initiated.

In a third model, circumstance or the environment are held responsible for the problem but the person is held responsible for the solution, ('the society got us into this mess . . . but only you and I can get us out of it'; this is termed the 'compensatory model'). Thus, past fit is more likely to be seen as E-initiated and future fit is more likely to be seen as P-initiated.

The fourth model views the person as responsible both for the problem and its resolution (termed the 'moral model'; for example, Est therapy which became well-known in the 1970s). Persons who hold this model will view past and future fit as P-initiated.

The four models provide an organized way for characterizing whether past combinations of P and E will predict to similar or dissimilar combinations of anticipated P and E. For example, suppose that retrospections of past PE fit are viewed as past 'problems' by a person holding the compensatory model, the environment is responsible for the problem but self is responsible for the solution. Then, the person's retrospection of past misfit should be based on a view that the misfit was E-initiated or initiated by circumstance and that the future, which should provide good fit, will be P-initiated.

If the person does not view past misfit as past 'problems' but as past 'solutions', then the four models may not explain the person's anticipated levels of P and E. When past PE fit is viewed as past solutions by the person, the degree of fit represents levels of achievement and a history of success (or failure). In that case, one would predict that the person's anticipation of future abilities (P_a) and of commensurate environmental demands (E_a) would be similar to the person's retrospected abilities and demands to the extent that the person perceived: (a) ability (P) to be relatively stable, and (b) the demands of the anticipated environment (E) to be relatively similar to demands of the past.

Discussion and Summary

PE fit and the buffering effect of social support

Social support can be viewed as the communication of liking, trust, respect or esteem, affirmation of one's beliefs and perceptions, and certain kinds of direct assistance (e.g., Katz and Kahn, 1978). Evidence indicates that social support is inversely related to emotional strain (e.g., Vanfossen, 1981; House, 1981; Abbey, Abramis and Caplan, 1981; Caplan, *et al.*, 1980) and physiological strain (Berkman and Syme, 1979). It is positively related to health-related coping (e.g., Shinn, *et al.*, 1977; Caplan, *et al.*, 1980), and appears to buffer the harmful effects of stressors in some cases (e.g., Cobb, 1976; House and Wells, 1978; Kadushin, Boulanger, and Martin, 1981) but not in others (e.g. Frydman, 1981; Pinneau, 1975).

Where buffering does occur, the actual psychological mechanisms by which it has its effects are not understood. A number of pathways by which social support might have its buffering effects are described in Caplan (1979). These pathways deal primarily with the effects of social support on components of motivation to respond to PE misfit.

The elaborated model of PE fit identifies additional points of intervention where social support can have buffering effects. These points of intervention deal with retrospected and anticipated fit. The rationale for buffering is as follows.

The elaborated model of PE fit contains the hypotheses that retrospected fit and anticipated fit influence the subjective meaning of current subjective fit. Retrospections provide the person with a gauge by which to judge the extent to which current subjective fit is an improvement, worsening, or no change compared to past fit. Accordingly, retrospections are expected to influence the effect of current subjective fit on strain. Anticipated fit can make the current level of fit appear more, less, or equally desirable compared to the fit anticipated, and accordingly, anticipations also should influence the effect of current subjective fit on strain. By deduction, social support that is aimed at the components of retrospected and anticipated fit should alter the relationship between current subjective fit and strain.

Such support would be directed at increasing the person's esteem and would involve the communication of respect for the person and the person's abilities. For example, a counsellor or friend may tell the person 'look, you don't give yourself enough credit for how much you accomplished since you first started dealing with this problem' (an attempt to modify retrospected fit and its relationship to current subjective fit). Or the person may be told 'You underestimate your ability to handle such responsibility. I know you will be able to handle the demands' (an attempt to modify the P_s component of anticipated fit).

Response certainty and time perspective in PE fit

Methodological issues. Self-report measures are usually constructed under the assumption that the response task falls within most respondent's abilities. There is always the possibility, however, that the respondent may be uncertain about how to answer a self-report measure. For measures of subjective PE fit, this uncertainty seems likely to increase as the person is asked to retrospect further back or further forward in time. Holding time from the present constant, retrospections should be subject to less of this uncertainty than anticipations. For retrospections the person is most likely to already have the requested response information. On the other hand, anticipations, by definition, deal with expectations rather than with empirically established certainties.

If these hypothesized effects are the case, then the hypothesized effects of retrospected and anticipated fit described in the elaborated model will tend to be confounded with the response uncertainty. To unconfound these effects, it may be desirable to assess the response uncertainty surrounding each parameter. This is not a methodological paper, so only brief mention will be made of some methods of assessing such uncertainty.

One could assess response uncertainty directly via rating scales ('How uncertain/certain are you about this rating?') or by allowing the respondent to indicate a bandwidth of response on the scales of P and E (e.g., 'I think my future responsibility for the well-being of others will be between 3 and 5'). One might also be able to infer response uncertainty by measuring within-person differences in latency of response (e.g., Markus, 1977; La Barbera and MacLachlin, 1979) to different PE fit questions (this might be done by presenting items on a video display terminal and timing the latency until the respondent entered a rating on the keyboard of the terminal).

Response uncertainty and certainty as stressors. The degree of response uncertainty should be of interest for substantive as well as analytic reasons relating to the PE fit model. For one thing, uncertainty about the future is a stressor associated with anxiety (e.g., Archer, 1979; Phares, 1973). Consequently, uncertainty with regard to anticipated misfit should be associated with anxiety. These effects should be greatest for persons with a high intolerance of ambiguity (Frenkel-Brunswik, 1949; Kahn, *et al.*, 1964).

The other end of the uncertainty continuum, certainty, may also have strain-producing effects that should be identified. People with a preference for ambiguity in their lives ('I hate a routine. I never know what tomorrow will bring, and I like it that way.') may find certainty about the future strain-producing. The certainty that things will be bad may lead to feelings of helplessness and depression (Arieti, 1970).

If one assumes that anticipated PE misfit, particularly a large amount of misfit, is undesirable, then the more *certain* one is that the misfit will occur, the more strain-producing the misfit will be. This follows from the learned helplessness literature. Although there is debate about the determinants of learned helplessness in humans, e.g., Wortman and Dintzer, 1978), evidence suggests that depression is associated with expectancies that the future will be both undesirable and unalterable (e.g., Abramson, *et al.*, 1978). The extent to which depression is the result of these cognitions, precedes them, or is part of a causal loop with them remains to be resolved.

Strategies for testing the elaborated model

The measurement of F_o is essential for distinguishing between defence and coping, (French, *et al.*, 1974), and for understanding the unique effects of intrapsychic and environmental determinants of human adjustment and environmental mastery. The difficulties of measuring F_o and F_s along commensurate dimensions in field situations will probably not disappear in the near future. Consequently, it may be useful to devote some attention to laboratory experiments where measures of F_o can be obtained more easily and compared with commensurate measures of F_s (e.g., Sales, 1969).

At the same time, several questions regarding the PE fit model can continue to be pursued in field settings. These questions deal with relationships among the subjective parameters of the model. A series of studies, associated with the ISR Social Environment and Health Program, are exploring some of these subjective parameters. One study (in collaboration with R. K. Naidu and R. C. Tripathi of the University of Allahabad) is examining the relative influence of past, present, and anticipated subjective fit in academic life in India on psychological strain and physical health. Two other studies (one in collaboration with D. Abramis; one by S. Doehrman and J. R. P. French, Jr.) are examining the contrast effects of past versus current versus anticipated social support and use of skills and abilities on emotional strains in work and marriage and on general affects. The Doehrman and French study includes several measures of PE fit.

Another study (in collaboration with A. Abbey, D. Abramis, F. Andrews, T. Conway, and J. R. P. French, Jr.) is examining changes in current PE fit regarding control over emotions and personal life as a function of: (a) anxiolytic treatment with diazepam (Valium), and (b) other modes of response to stressors. The study is collecting data from four waves of interviews spaced six weeks apart. The study is unique in that it is also gathering four sets of retrospective data ranging from one to about six weeks of retrospection. The retrospective data assesses perceived quality of life, anxiety, and tranquillizer use, but does not deal with stressors assessed via PE fit. Nevertheless, the set of 24 retrospections are expected to help us test hypotheses about the role of retrospections on current perceptions, about the predictors of retrospective biases in cognition, and about the role of retrospection on well-being.

From this set of studies, and hopefully from the future research of others, we may be able to determine the extent to which links in models such as the one in Figure 5 are plausible. It is likely that these studies will discount the influence of some pathways and suggest new links and new concepts not considered (the heuristic of drawing all possible links in Figure 5 or between P and E components in an expanded model of Figure 5 has not been carried out).

It may be that a more highly evolved model will eventually confront us with Bonini's paradox — the more realistic and detailed the model, the more it resembles the organization of what it attempts to model, including 'resemblance in the directions of incomprehensibility and indescribability' (Starbuck, 1976, p. 1101). For now the risk seems minor. If there is any incomprehensibility at this point, it is hopefully more the result of the model than of the phenomena set out for study.

Summary

Studies of PE fit have focused largely on subjective perceptions of current fit. These studies have explained statistically significant amounts of variance in strain not already accounted for by *P* and *E* additively. Nevertheless, the amount of variance in strain explained by PE fit has not been large in absolute terms, although it has doubled the amount of variance explained. To increase the predictive power of PE fit theory may require an elaboration of the current model. The elaboration, presented here, is based on the core theory and concepts of French, *et al.* (1974). The major additions in the elaborated model are the concepts of retrospected and nonretrospected past fit and future, anticipated fit. The text presents hypothetical examples of data to demonstrate how the joint consideration of PE fit in the past, present, and anticipated future time frames may increase the explanatory power of PE fit theory.

The elements of the elaborated model provide the basis for several hypotheses. These hypotheses state that retrospected and anticipated fit have both main as well as interactive effects on strain.

The cognitive elements of the model serve as hypothesized determinants of subjective current and anticipated fit. These elements should make it possible to detail some of the biasing mechanisms that produce discrepancies between subjective and objective fit.

Finally, a distinction is made between P-initiated and E-initiated changes in *P* and *E*. This distinction is proposed in order to increase the ability of the model to predict conditions under which no change in fit may be strain-producing and under which an attainment of PE fit may be strain-producing. These distinctions are compatible with the original propositions of PE fit theory. They allow one to deal with cases where the degree of fit on one dimension may influence the degree of fit (misfit) on other dimensions important to the person.

References

Abbey, A., Abramis, D. J., and Caplan, R. D. (August, 1981) Measuring social support: The effects of frame of reference on the relationship between social support and strain. Paper presented at the Eighty-ninth Annual Convention of the Amercian Psychological Association. Available from A. Abbey, Institute for Social Research, Ann, Arbor, Michigan.

Abramson, L. Y., Garber, J., Edwards, N. B., and Seligman, M. E. P. (1978) Expectancy changes in depression and schizophrenia. *Journal of Abnormal Psychology*, **87**, 102–9.

Abramson, L. Y., Seligman, M. E. P., and Teasdale, J. D. (1978) Learned helplessness in humans: Critique and reformulation. *Journal of Abnormal Psychology*, **87**, 49–74.

Adams, J. S. (1965) Inequity in social exchange. In L. Berkowitz (Ed.), *Advances in Social Psychology*. New York: Academic Press, 267–299.

Archer, R. P. (1979) Relationships between locus of control and anxiety. *Journal of Personality Assessment*, **43**, 617–26.

Arieti, S. (1970) Cognition and feeling. In M. Arnold (Ed.), *Feelings and Emotions*. New York: Academic Press, 135–44.

Asch, S. (1956) Studies of independence and conformity. I. A minority of one against a unanimous majority. *Psychological Monographs*, **70** (Whole No. 416).

Atkinson, J. W., and Feather, N. T. (1966) *A Theory of Achievement Motivation*, New York: Wiley.

Beck, A. T. (1976) *Cognitive Therapy and the Emotional Disorders*. New York: International Universities Press.

Berkman, L. F., and Syme, S. L. (1979) Social networks, host resistance, and mortality: A nine-year follow-up study of Alameda County residents. *American Journal of Epidemiology*, **109**, 186–204.

Bowers, K. S. (1973) Situationism in psychology: an analysis and a critique. *Psychological Review*, **80**, 307–36.

Brehm, J. W. (1966) *A Theory of Psychological Reactance*. New York: Academic Press.

Brickman, P., and Campbell, D. T. (1971) Hedonic relativism and planning the good society. In M. H. Appley (Ed.), *Adaptation Level Theory*. New York: Academic Press, 287–304.

Brickman, P., Rabinowitz, V. C., Coates, D., Cohn, E., Kidder, L., and Karuza, J (1982). Helping. *American Psychologist*, **37**, 368–384.

Brown, J. S. (1948) Gradients of approach and avoidance responses and their relation to motivation. *Journal of Comparative and Physiological Psychology*, **41**, 450–65.

Burger, J. M. and Cooper, H. M. (1979) The desirability of control. *Motivation and Emotion*, **3**, 381–93.

Cannell, C. F., Fisher, G., and Baker, T. (1965) Reporting of hospitalization in the heatlh interview survey. *Vital and Health Statistics*, Series 2, No. 5. Washington, D. C.: U.S. Public Health Service.

Cannell, C. F., Miller, P. V., and Oksenberg, L. (1981) Research on interviewing techniques. In S. Leinhardt (Ed.), *Sociological Methodology, 1981*. San Francisco: Jossey-Bass, 389–38.

Cantril, H. (1938) The prediction of social events. *Journal of Abnormal and Social Psychology*, **33**, 364–89.

Caplan, R. D. (1971) Organizational stress and individual strain: A social-psychological study of risk factors in coronary heart disease among administrators, engineers, and scientists (Doctoral dissertation, The University of Michigan). (University Microfilms No. 72–14822).

Caplan, R. D. (1979) Social support, person–environment fit, and coping. In L. Ferman and J. Gordus (Eds), *Mental Health and the Economy*. Kalamazoo, Mich.: W. E. Upjohn Institute for Employment Research.

Caplan, R. D., Cobb, S., French, J. R. P., Jr., Harrison, R. V., and Pinneau, S. R. (1980) *Job Demands and Worker Health: Main Effects and Occupational Differences*. Ann Arbor, Mich.: Institute for Social Research.

Caplan, R. D., Harrison, R. V., Wellons, R. V., and French, J. R. P., Jr. (1980)

Social support and patient adherence: Experimental and survey findings. Ann Arbor: Institute for Social Research, Research Report Series.

Cobb, S. (1976) Social support as a moderator of life stress. *Psychosomatic Medicine*, **3**, 300–14.

Conway, T. L., Abbey, A., and French, J. R. P. Jr. (1982) Perceptions of control in different life domains. Unpublished manuscript, Ann Arbor: Institute for Social Research, January.

Cronbach, L. J., and Furby, L. (1970) How should we measure 'change' — or should we? *Psychological Bulletin*, **74**, 68–80.

deCharms, R. (1968) *Personal Causation: The Internal Affective Determinants of Behaviour.* New York: Academic Press.

Ericcson, K. A., and Simon, H. A. (1980) Verbal reports as data. *Psychological Review*, **87**, 215–51.

Feather, N. T., and Davenport, P. R. (1981) Unemployment and depressive affect: a motivational and attributional analysis. *Journal of Personality and Social Psychology*, **41**, 422–36.

Festinger, L. (1954) A theory of social comparison processes. *Human Relations*, **12**, 147–62.

Fischoff, B. (1975) Hindsight = foresight: The effect of outcome knowledge on judgement under uncertainty. *Journal of Experimental Psychology: Human Perception and Performance*, **1**, 288–99.

Fishbein, M., Raven, B. H., and Hunter, R. (1963) Social comparison and dissonance reduction in self evaluation. *Journal of Abnormal and Social Psychology*, **67**, 491–501.

Frankenhaeuser, M. (1980) Psychoendocrine approaches to the study of stressful person-environment transactions. In H. Selye (Ed.), *Selye's Guide to Stress Research* (Vol. 1). New York: Van Nostrand.

French, J. R. P., Jr., and Caplan, R. D. (1972) Organizational stress and individual strain. In A. Marrow (Ed.), *The Failure of Success.* New York: AMACOM.

French, J. R. P., Jr., Caplan, R. D., and Harrison, R. V. (In press). *The Mechanisms of Job Stress and Strain.* London: Wiley.

French, J. R. P., Jr., and Raven, B. (1959) The bases of social power. In D. Cartwright (Ed.), *Studies in Social Power.* Ann Arbor, Mich.: Institute for Social Research, 150–167.

French, J. R. P., Jr., Rodgers, W., and Cobb, S. (1974) Adjustment as person–environment fit. In G. V. Coelho, D. A. Hamburg, and J. E. Adams (Eds), *Coping and Adaptation.* New York: Basic Books.

Frenkel-Brunswik, E. (1949) Intolerance of ambiguity as an emotional and perceptual personality variable. *Journal of Personality*, **18**, 108–43.

Frydman, M. I. (1981) Social support, life events and psychiatric symptoms: A study of direct, conditional and interaction effects. *Social Psychiatry*, **16**, 69–78.

Glass, D. (1977) *Behaviour Patterns, Stress, and Coronary Disease.* Hillsdale, New Jersey: Lawrence Erlbaum.

Harrison, R. V. (1976) Job demands and worker health: Person–environment misfit (Doctoral dissertation, The University of Michigan, 1976). *Dissertation Abstracts International*, **37**, 1035B.

Harrison, R. V. (1978) Person–environment fit and job stress. In C. L. Cooper and R. Payne (Eds), *Stress at Work.* New York: Wiley.

Harvey, J. H., Ickes, W. J., and Kidd, R. F. (Eds) (1976). *New Directions in Attribution Research* (Vol. 1). Hillsdale, New Jersey: Erlbaum.

Helson, H. (1948) Adaptation-level as a basis for a quantitative theory of frames of reference. *Psychological Review*, **55**, 297–313.

Holmes, D. S. (1970) Differential change in affective intensity and forgetting of unpleasant personal experience. *Journal of Personality and Social Psychology*, **15**, 234–9.

House, J. S. (1972) The relationship of intrinsic and extrinsic work motivations to occupational stress and coronary heart disease risk. Doctoral dissertation, The University of Michigan. *Dissertation Abstracts International*, **33**, 2514A (University of Microfilms No. 72–29084).

House, J. S. (1981) *Work Stress and Social Support*. Reading, Mass.: Addison-Wesley.

House, J. S., and Wells, J. A. (1978) Occupational stress, social support, and health. In A. McLean, G. Black, and M. Colligan (Eds), *Reducing occupational stress: Proceedings of a conference* (HEW Publication No. (NIOSH) 78–140). Washington, D.C.: U.S. Department of Health, Education, and Welfare.

Houston, B. K. (1977) Dispositional anxiety and the effectiveness of cognitive strategies in stressful laboratory and classroom situations. In C. D. Spielberger and I. B. Sarason (Eds), *Stress and Anxiety* (Vol. 4). New York: Wiley.

Jahoda, M. (1958) *Current Concepts of Positive Mental Health*. New York: Basic Books.

Janis, I. L. (1962) Psychological effects of warnings. In G. W. Baker and D. W. Chapman (Eds), *Man and Society in Disaster*. New York: Basic Books, Inc. Publishers, 55–92.

Janoff-Bulman, R. (1979) Characterological versus behavioural self-blame: Inquiries into depression and rape. *Journal of Personality and Social Psychology*, **37**, 1798–809.

Janoff-Bulman, R., and Brickman, P. (1982) Expectations and what people learn from failure. In N. T. Feather (Ed.), *Expectations and Actions*. Hillsdale, New Jersey: Lawrence Erlbaum Associates, 207–37.

Joreskog, K. G., and Sorbom, D. (1977) Statistical models and methods for analysis of longitudinal data. In D. J. Aigner and A. S. Goldberger (Eds) *Latent Variables in Socioeconomic Models*. Amsterdam: North Holland Publishing Co., 285–325.

Kadushin, C., Boulanger, G., and Martin, J. (1981) Long term stress reactions: some causes, consequences, and naturally occurring support systems. In A. Egendorf, C. Kadushin, R. S. Lauger, G. Rothbart, and L. Sloan (Eds), *Legacies of Vietnam: Comparative Adjustment of Veterans and their Peers*. Washington: U.S. Government Printing Office, House Committee Print No. 14, 475–706.

Kahana, E., Liang, J., and Felton, B. J. (1980) Alternative models of person–environment fit: Prediction of morale in three homes for the aged. *Journal of Gerontology*, **35**, 584–95.

Kahn, R. L., Wolfe, D. M., Quinn, R. P., Snoek, J. D., and Rosenthal, R. A. (1964) *Organizational Stress: Studies in Role Conflict and Ambiguity*. New York: Wiley.

Katz, D., and Kahn, R. L. (1978) *The Social Psychology of Organizations*. New York: Wiley.

Kenny, D. A. (1979) *Correlation and Causality*. New York: Wiley.

Kraut, A. (1965) The study of role conflicts and their relationships to job satisfaction, tension, and performance (Doctoral dissertation, University of Michigan). *Dissertation Abstracts*, **26**, 7476. (University Microfilms, No. 66–6637).

Kulka, R. A. (1975) Person–environment fit in the high school: A validation study (2 vols) (Doctoral dissertation, University of Michigan, 1975). *Dissertation Abstracts International*, 1976, **36**, 5352B (University Microfilms, No. 76–9438).

Kulka, R. A. (1979) Interaction as person–environment fit. *New Directions for Methodology of Behavioral Science, 2,* 55–71.

Kulka, R. W., Klingel, D. M., and Mann, D. W. (1980) School crime and disruption as a function of student shcool fit: An empirical assessment. *Journal of Youth and Adolescence,* **9,** 353–70.

Kulka, R. W., Mann, D. W., and Klingel, D. M. (1980) A person–environment fit model of school crime and disruption. In K. Baker and R. J. Rubel (Eds), *Violence and Crime in the Schools: Theoretical Perspectives.* Lexington-Heath, 49–60.

La Barbera, P. A., and MacLachlin, J. M. (1979) Response latency in telephone interviews. *Journal of Advertising Research,* **19,** 49–55.

Langer, E. J. (1975) The illusion of control. *Journal of Personality and Social Psychology,* **32,** 311–28.

Langer, E. J., and Rodin, J. (1976) The effects of choice and enhanced personal responsibility for the aged: A field experiment in an institutional setting. *Journal of Personality and Social Psychology,* **34,** 191–8.

Lazarus, R. S. (1966) *Psychological Stress and the Coping Process.* New York: McGraw-Hill.

Lazarus, R. S. (1979) Positive denial: The case for not facing reality. *Psychology Today,* November, 44–60.

Lazarus, R. S., and Averill, J. R. (1972) Emotion and cognition: with special reference to anxiety. In Spielberger, C. D. (Ed.), *Anxiety. Current Trends in Theory and Research* (Vol. II). New York: Academic Press, 242–84.

Lefcourt, H. M. (1973) The function of the illusions of control and freedom. *American Psychologist,* **28,** 417–25.

Levine, R. V., West, L. K., and Reis, H. T. (1980) Perceptions of time and punctuality in the United States and Brazil. *Journal of Personality and Social Psychology,* **38,** 541–550.

Lewin, K. (1935) *A Dynamic Theory of Personality.* New York: McGraw-Hill.

Lewin, K. (1942) Field theory of learning. *Yearbook of the National Society for the Study of Education, 41,* Part II, 215–42.

Lewin, K. (1951) *Field Theory in Social Science.* D. Cartwright (Ed.) New York: Harper & Row.

McGrath, J. E. (1976) Stress and behavior in organizations. In M. D. Dunnette (Ed.), *Handbook of Industrial and Organizational Psychology.* Chicago: Rand McNally, 1351–96.

McGregor, D. (1938) The major determinants of the prediction of social events. *Journal of Abnormal and Social Psychology,* **33,** 179–204.

McKennell, A. C. and Andrews, F. M. (1980) Models of cognition and affect in perceptions of well-being. *Social Indicators Research,* **8,** 257–98.

March, J. G., and Simon, H. A. (1958) *Organizations.* New York: Wiley.

Markus, H. (1977) Self-schemata and processing information about the self. *Journal of Personality and Social Psychology,* **35,** 63–78.

Merton, R. K., and Kitt, A. S. (1950) Contributions to the theory of reference group behaviour. In R. K. Merton and P. F. Lazarsfeld (Eds), *Continuities in Social Research: Studies in the Scope and Method of 'The American Soldier.'* Glencoe, Illinois: Free Press of Glencoe.

Milburn, M. A. (1978) Sources of bias in the prediction of future events. *Organizational Behavior and Human Performance,* **21,** 17–26.

Miller, D. T., and Porter, C. A. (1980) Effects of temporal perspective on the attribution process. *Journal of Personality and Social Psychology,* **38,** 532–41.

Miller, S. M. (1979) Controllability and human stress: Method, evidence and theory. *Behaviour Research and Therapy*, **17**, 287–304.

Mills, R. T., and Krantz, D. S. (1979) Information, choice, and reactions to stress: A field experiment in a blood bank with laboratory analogue. *Journal of Personality and Social Psychology*, **17**, 287–304.

Murray, H. A. (1938) *Explorations in Personality*. New York: Oxford University Press.

Nisbett, R. E., and Ross, L. (1980). *Human Inference: Strategies and Shortcomings of Social Judgement*. Englewood Cliffs, New Jersey: Prentice-Hall.

Pervin, L. A. (1967a) Satisfaction and perceived self-environment similarity: A semantic differential study of student-college interaction. *Journal of Personality*, **35**, 623–34.

Pervin, L. A. (1967b) A twenty-college study of student × college interaction using TAPE (transactional analysis of personality and environment): Rationale, reliability, and validity. *Journal of Educational Psychology*, **58**, 290–302.

Pervin, L. A. (1968) Performance and satisfaction as a function of individual-environment fit. *Psychological Bulletin*, **69**, 56–68.

Peterson, C., Schwartz, S. M. and Seligman, M. E. P. (1981) Self-blame and depressive symptoms. *Journal of Personality and Social Psychology*, **41**, 253–9.

Phares, E. J. (1973) *Locus of Control: A Personality Determinant of Behavior*. Morristown, N. J.: General Learning Press.

Pinneau, S. R., Jr. (1975) Effects of social support on psychological and physiological strain. (Doctoral dissertation, University of Michigan) Ann Arbor, Mich.: University Microfilms, 1975, No. 76–9491.

Rommetveit, R. (1954) *Social Norms and Roles*. Minneapolis: University of Minnesota Press.

Ross, C. E., and Mirowsky, J. III (1979) A comparison of life-event-weighting schemes: change, undesirability, and effect-proportional indices. *Journal of Health and Social Behavior*, **20**, 166–77.

Sales, S. M. (1969) Organizational role as a risk factor in coronary disease. *Administrative Science Quarterly*, **14**, 325–336.

Seligman, M. E. P. (1975) *Helplessness: On Depression, Helplessness, and Death*. San Francisco: Freeman.

Seligman, M. E. P., Maier, S. F., and Solomon, R. L. (1971) Unpredictable and uncontrollable aversive events. In F. R. Brush (Ed.), *Aversive Conditioning and Learning*. New York: Academic Press.

Sherwood, J. J. (1965) Self-identity and referent others. *Sociometry*, **28**, 66–81.

Shinn, M., Caplan, R. D., Robinson, E. A. R., French, J. R. P., Jr. and Caldwell, J. R. (1977) Advances in antihypertensive adherence: social support and patient education. *Urban Health*, **6**(20), (21), 57–9.

Starbuck, W. H. (1976) Organizations and their environments. In M. D. Dunnette (Ed), *Handbook of Industrial and Organizational Psychology*. Chicago: Rand McNally, 1069–123.

Tannenbaum, A. S., and Kuleck, W. J. Jr. (1978) The effect on organization members of discrepancy between perceived and preferred rewards implicit in work. *Human Relations*, **31**, 809–22.

Thompson, S. C. (1981) Will it hurt less if I can control it? A complex answer to a simple question. *Psychological Bulletin*, **90**, 89–101.

Tversky, A., and Kahneman, D. (1973) Availability; a heuristic for judging frequency. *Cognitive Psychology*, **5**, 207–32.

Vanfossen, B. E. (1981) Sex differences in the mental health effects of social support and equity. *Journal of Health and Social Behavior*, **22**, 130–43.

Wanous, J. P., and Lawler, E. E., III (1972) Measurement and meaning of job satisfaction. *Journal of Applied Psychology*, **56**, 95–105.

Wortman, C. B., and Dintzer, L. (1978) Is an attributional analysis of the learned helplessness phenomenon viable?: A critique of the Abramson–Seligman–Teasdale Reformation. *Journal of Abnormal Psychology*, **87**, 75–90.

Notes

1. Work on this article was supported by funding from Hoffmann-La Roche and by NIMH Grant R01 MH34586. The author would like to thank Antonia Abbey, John R. P. French, Jr., Rama C. Tripathi, and Richard W. Kulka for their comments and suggestions. Mary Jo Griewahn performed the word processing for the original manuscript using the University of Michigan TEXTEDIT-MTS software system.

2. The theory has been concerned with fit between conditions external to the person (E) but it could be adapted to consider person–person fit, such as the fit between the amount of discomfort the person experiences due to an illness and the amount that the person is willing to tolerate.

3. In brief, one can transform PE fit scores to represent linearly scaled variables so that methods of analysis assuming linear relationships, such as regression, can be used. The U-shaped curve can be transformed by taking the absolute difference between P and E items or indices. The asymptotic curve can be transformed with an approximation as follows. If one hypothesizes that only $P>E$ produces strain, then scores of $P>E$ are kept in their original metric whereas scores of $P=E$ or $P<E$ are transformed to zero. If one hypothesizes that only $P<E$ produces strain, then scores of $P<E$ are kept in their original metric whereas scores of $P=E$ and $P>E$ are set to zero. Finally, the linear curve (curve C) need not be transformed at all. It can be represented in multiple regression analyses as the additive effects of P and of E. Other methods of considering P and E jointly, such as ratios, are evaluated by Kulka (1979) and Harrison (1976).

4. Those hypotheses and examples which have been framed in terms of changes are not intended to imply the use of change scores or any particular psychometric operations by which changes would be assessed. It has been demonstrated that computed change scores, in some instances, can be unreliable (Cronbach and Furby, 1970), and that there are modelling techniques, such as multiple regression of initial and final scores, that can be used to represent the degree of change. This paper does not deal with the statistical modelling of these hypotheses. For a discussion of analytic procedures see Kenny (1979) or Joreskog and Sorbom (1977).

In examining change in fit, one could evaluate the gain or loss of fit as a ratio of present fit to past fit. In that way, for example, one could entertain predictions such as the following: a gain of $1000 for a millionaire will be perceived as less strain-reducing than it would be for a person who is a pauper. The use of such ratio scales requires data such as income with a true zero point. Harrison (1976) has conducted cross-sectional analyses of how PE fit on income affects strain, although data on perceived change have not been reported in any studies so far.

5. A set of notations for making this specification might look like the following: $E_{e3,tx-ty}$ = a change in E, initiated by E between tx and ty; $E_{p,tx-ty}$ = a change in E, initiated by P between tx and ty.

6. An effort to integrate theories of PE fit and of attribution is now underway (Conway, Abbey, and French, 1982). The study is examining the amount of control

people perceive to be held by others, chance, and self, and the amount of control they prefer to be held by others, chance, and self. The study is examining the generalizability of PE fit on attributions of control across several domains such as work and personal life. The study is also examining the relationship of fit on the attributions to coping, including the use of minor tranquillizers, affective well-being, and perceived quality of life.

Stress Research
Edited by Cary L. Cooper
© 1983, John Wiley & Sons, Ltd.

Chapter 4
Pursuing the Link Between Stressful Life Experiences and Disease: A Time for Reappraisal

Stanislav V. Kasl
Professor of Epidemiology, Yale University School of Medicine, USA

Introduction

Unquestionably, research on the stress–disease connection has a high marquee value: it has engrossed many an investigator and it has captured the attention of mass media and the general public. Thus an evaluation of progress in the field need not be greatly concerned with the possibility that a methodological critique will prematurely threaten the survival of a worthwhile scientific hypothesis, or that the scientific and lay communities are inadequately sensitized to the possibility that certain situations or experiences may have adverse health consequences. The possible link between stress and disease has received a generous airing and a hard-nosed examination of evidence, of progress and of accomplishments, is unlikely to be destructive.

It is illuminating to compare the two edited volumes on stressful life events which came out in 1974 and 1981 (Dohrenwend and Dohrenwend, 1974; and 1981a). The earlier volume had a large section which dealt with content (review of evidence, reports of empirical findings) and a small section on methodology. The more recent volume is overwhelmingly methodological, with a secondary emphasis on theoretical issues; empirical findings from new studies are practically invisible. Assuming that this is not merely a reflection of the idiosyncratic proclivities of the editors, we may well question the significance of this unusual trajectory of scientific progress. Does it suggest, for example, that current and near-future research accomplishments are to be demarcated and denoted by methodological improvements, and that at present, additions to the empirical data base are likely to be both premature and flawed? Does it, in fact, mean that at the moment, methodological research should replace substantive research until our methodology is well 'in place'?

In this chapter, I wish to explore and defend the validity of the following interrelated arguments: (1) Stressful life events must be conceptualized, to a greater extent, as characteristics of the person rather than as a separate (and separable) characteristic of the person's environment; this has serious consequences for research design strategies which seek to detect and define the aetiological role of stressful life experiences. (2) Past and current methodological criticisms and research have emphasized measurement issues rather than causal-aetiological problems; this emphasis on measurement is a displacement to a secondary, albeit more manageable, problem (analogous to looking for one's lost car keys under the street light, where one can see better, rather than in the dark alley, where the keys were lost). (3) The current disquietude regarding methods and knowledge in the area of stressful life events and disease is in no small part attributable to the availability of a simple short instrument, namely the Schedule of Recent Experience, SRE (Hawkins et al., 1957), and the many modifications and variations on this early instrument (e.g., Dohrenwend et al., 1978; Holmes and Rahe, 1967; Horowitz et al., 1977; Hurst et al., 1978; Paykel et al., 1971; Rahe, 1978). Through the uncritical but widespread use of these lists of 'stressful life events', a flood of studies has been created, which have a momentum of their own, which demand that we attend to the issues which they have created, and which sidetrack us from the main objective, understanding the life events–disease aetiology. Some of the secondary issues raised are: Does the instrument measure stress? How shall we weigh the events? How reliable is the recall? Should desirable events be included? etc. The SRE-type instrument is, in fact, devastatingly unsuitable for the orderly and detailed study of the aetiological role of stressful life experiences in disease and of the possible mechanisms involved.

The above three arguments are intended to increase the level of scepticism toward past research and to influence the direction of future studies. I recognize, of course, that quasi-experimental field research on the disease impact of stressful life situations and experiences is carried out under considerable ethical, practical, and scientific constraints. In particular, absence of experimental control over possible confounding variables in the real-life field setting precludes clear-cut causal interpretations. As a consequence, feasible and actual research designs are always compromises some distance away from the scientific ideal, and methodological criticisms of such actual designs are, in some sense, 'unfair' and unrealistic. I shall, therefore, endeavour to develop and elaborate the above arguments within these practical constraints on field research which perforce influence every investigator.

In 1974, Mechanic (1974) offered the following summary of the extent of our knowledge: 'it is clear that stressful life events play some role in the occurrence of illness in populations. But any statement beyond this vague generalization is likely to stir controversy' (p. 87). This statement is marvelously vague and precise at the same time, and it captured nicely the sense of the evidence as of 1974. By 1981, we have become clearer about the nature of our ignorance, but our knowledge base has apparently not changed. For example, causal models and path-analytic methods (Dohrenwend and Dohrenwend, 1981b; Golden and Dohrenwend, 1981) have been offered, which systematize our ignorance and usefully clarify the different ways in which life events could contribute to the broader complex aetiological picture. Enhancing the pedagogic usefulness of these models is the fact that they include three important possibilities: (a) no aetiological role for life events; (b) life events entering in spurious associations only; and (c) life events as a consequence of health status changes. These possibilities must be the starting point for reviews of evidence and for research design planning.

A Note on 'Stress'

The term 'stress' continues to be used in several fundamentally different ways: (a) as an environmental condition; (b) as an appraisal of an environmental situation; (c) as the response to that condition; and (d) as some form of relationship between the environmental demands and the person's ability to meet the demands. Furthermore, within each of these broad categories of usage, many definitions of stress abound. Given this situation, it would seem that one cannot make much progress in the stress field until investigators agree on definitions, achieve greater conceptual precision, and improve on the operational methodology. In this paper, however, I wish to take the position that the aetiological role of stressful life experiences in disease can be examined and discussed without having to improve on the term 'stress' beyond its loose and imprecise vernacular usage. The more specific questions we can propose and answer, the less we have a need for the troublesome and recalcitrant concept of stress: Which life events have adverse health consequences? Which do not? Why the difference? What biological mechanisms are involved? What is the role of behavioural variables and psychological processes? Other questions like: Does the SRE measure stress? What makes events stressful (e.g., undesirability vs. change)? When does stress lead to disease outcomes? — may or may not be meaningful, but they do not appear essential to the business at hand.

The Aetiological Perspective of Psychosocial Epidemiology

The primary question in this chapter is: What is the aetiological role of stressful life experiences in disease onset and /or exacerbation, and how can we best investigate this role? Stated somewhat differently: Are stressful life experiences risk factors for disease outcomes? The perspective of epidemiology is a useful one not only because of the traditional emphasis on agent–host–environment (Susser, 1981a), but also because of epidemiology's long history of methodological developments in multi-factorial aetiological research on disease and the possible role of psychosocial, as distinct from biological, risk factors. Three notions from epidemiology are pertinent here: (a) the interplay of biological and psychosocial risk factors; (b) stages of disease development; and (c) the concept of prospective study design.

There is no question that the preferred research strategy in prospective studies of psychosocial risk factors for a particular disease is to include in the initial data collection an assessment of the biological risk factors. The results of such a study are considerably more compelling when it is shown that a psychosocial variable is acting independently of (or synergistically with) established biological risk factors. Analyses of Type A Behaviour (Brand *et al.*, 1976), of low grade in civil servant occupations (Marmot *et al.*, 1978), and of occupational stresses in banking (Kittel *et al.*, 1980) as risk factors for coronary heart disease (CHD) are all made more convincing when the traditional cardiovascular risk factors are included as well. Failure to include them will often lead to improper conclusions, such as when one ignores that the association between stressful medical specialities and CHD rates (Russek, 1962) is largely explainable in terms of difference in cigarette smoking (Russek, 1965). It is not clear how many of the studies seeking to detect disease effects of stressful life experiences would have found it feasible to expand the design and include some biological risk factors, but the fact that so few past studies have done so suggests there is ample room for improvement.

When one starts out with a cohort which is not free of disease, then the need to assess biological risk factors is replaced by an even greater need to measure initial health status, morbidity, and comorbidity. A recent review of the empirical literature on course of disease (Kasl, 1982a) clearly reveals that without an adequate assessment of health status at the initial point from which course of disease is examined, detecting the causal role of stressful life events or other psychosocial variables becomes nearly impossible. Unfortunately, the pay-off from doing things right is often disappointment: when an adequate assessment of initial health status is made, one usually finds that it is a powerful predictor of subsequent health status and that intervening stressful life experiences seldom add much to that prediction.

The notion of stages of disease development can be quite useful in pinpointing the role of stressful life events or other psychosocial variables in health status changes. For a chronic disease such as CHD, the progression can be schematized as follows: (1) healthy, asymptomatic, risk factors absent; (2) asymptomatic, risk factor(s) present; (3) subclinical disease susceptible to detection (atherosclerosis; vascular stenoisis, occlusion); (4) initial symptom experience or initial episode of diagnosable illness; (5) course of disease, repeat episodes, exacerbations; (6) death (case fatality). When dealing with a distal outcome, such as elevated mortality after bereavement (Jacobs and

Ostfeld, 1977), this schema reminds us of the different ways the ulitmate outcome could have come about, such as through higher case fatality among those with disease, or higher incidence of new disease for a given level of risk factors, or changes in risk factors. Similarly, the schema of stages of disease development helps us to organize and interpret the data of sex differences in US CHD mortality (McGill and Stern, 1979): animal data on sex differences are inconsistent; diverse hormonal data do not point to any specific role of hormones; sex differences in risk factors cannot account for the sex differences in mortality; sex differences in atherosclerosis and in morbidity parallel those in mortality. This suggests overall, that the sex variable is better seen in social rather than biological terms, and that its influence seems to be pinpointed to the transition from risk factors to subclinical disease.

For infectious diseases, such as infectious mononucleosis (IM), the schema of stages of disease development are different from those for chronic conditions such as CHD: (1) initial immunity–susceptibility status; (2) exposure to infection among susceptibles; (3) development of inapparent vs. clinical illness among the exposed. The importance of such a schema pinpointing the role of psychosocial risk factors is seen in the analysis of one particular variable, strength of commitment to a military career, as a risk factor for IM among West Point cadets (Kasl *et al.*, 1979): those with stronger commitment were more likely to be susceptible at matriculation, were less likely to be infected during the 4 years at the Academy (among susceptibles), and were more likely to develop overt clinical IM (among infected). Thus one and the same variable was either a positive or a negative risk factor for IM, depending on the stage of the disease development process.

The concept of prospective study designs reminds us of the great vulnerability of retrospective case-control studies to a variety of alternative explanations of results. Consider, for example, the excellent case-control study of life events and depression carried out by Paykel *et al.* (1969): cases were a broadly representative sample of patients seeking treatment at a variety of community facilities and satisfying explicit criteria for depression, while controls came from a community probability sample and were matched on the appropriate socio-demographic characteristics. Nevertheless, the major finding—cases reporting more events than controls for the preceding 6 months (1.7 vs. 0.6)—is shrouded in ambiguity and major questions are left unanswered. Does the depressed status and the act of seeking help affect the recall and the reporting of life events? Can we disentangle onset of depression from onset of help-seeking? And, most importantly, can we really pin anything down with respect to the prior aetiological role of life events in ensuing depression with this design and the causal–temporal chain involved?

Requiems for retrospective life-event studies (Hudgen,s 1974) go unheard and calls for a moratorium on life-event research (Wershaw and Reinhart,

1974) go unanswered. Yet it is imperative that we face up to the question: will additional case-control retrospective studies add to our knowledge, no matter how many more are done, if they share the same weaknesses? The answer may well be 'no' for some well-explored conditions, though surely it is 'yes' for other diseases for which preliminary research of any kind is yet to be done. For example, it is reasonably clear that high levels of symptoms of anxiety, distress, or 'neuroticism' seem among myocardial infarction (MI) patients, compared to controls, are indicative of a post-MI effect and are not related prospectively to MI among people initially free of disease (Jenkins, 1976; Kasl, 1981). Thus it would be utterly unnecessary to carry out more case-control studies of MI and anxiety-distress and, indeed, the recent literature on cardiovascular epidemiology is mercifully free of such studies. (In fact, even in the absence of prospective studies which pinned down the role of anxiety in MI, additional retrospective studies would not have been useful, since the cross-sectional association was amply documented but remained causally ambiguous.) Retrospective accounts of pre-MI life conditions are also severely compromised by the finding that public beliefs about causes of heart attacks put 'stress, tension, pressure' considerably ahead of the conventional risk factors, such as high blood pressure and high cholesterol levels or cigarette smoking (Shekelle and Lin, 1978).

The need to commit ourselves courageously to the concept of prospective cohort studies is seen in critical reviews of literature which invariably point to the inconsistent and inadequate evidence emanating from case-control retrospective designs (e.g., Hurst *et al.*, 1976; Rabkin, 1980). Of course, not all circumstances call for prospective inquiry; for example, parental death in childhood as a risk factor for adult depressive disorders can be reasonably adequately examined retrospectively, as long as we are dealing with representative cases and controls and our assessment is appropriate. The recent consensus, incidentally, is that the risk factor relationship has not been established (Crook and Eliot, 1980; Tennant *et al.*, 1980).

The need for prospective studies is also seen in the disconcerting frequency with which apparently well-established evidence from case-control or cross-sectional studies fails to be supported by prospective data. For example, Goldberg and Comstock (1976) were unable to demonstrate any prospective association between life events and later hospitalizations or death in two separate community samples. In a prospective study of surgical patients (Rundall, 1978), life events revealed very weak and/or inconsistent relationships to post-surgery recovery. In a social experiment with negative income tax (Elesh and Lefcowitz, 1977), prospectively studied changes in income had little effect on various indicators of health status — in spite of the many cross-sectional associations between income and health. And one of the most solidly documented relationship, that between bereavement and increased mortality (e.g., Helsing and Szklo, 1981; Jacobs and Ostfeld, 1977; Rowland,

1977; Satariano and Syme, 1981; Susser, 1981b; Talbot *et al.*, 1981) is challenged by the findings of the two fully prospective studies (Fenwick and Barresi, 1981; Heyman and Gianturco, 1973) which failed to document health status deficits attributable to bereavement.

Prospective research designs have other benefits, such as enabling us to estimate the magnitude of the risk that a disorder will follow as a consequence of experiencing stressful life events (Dohrenwend and Dohrenwend, 1978). However, by far the most significant advantage is that such designs increase our chances of interpreting properly the causal–aetiological relationships. However, prospective studies do not guarantee this, by any means. I shall return to this important issue in a later section.

Are Stressful Life Experiences a Separable Characteristic of the Person's Environment?

There is little doubt that investigators in the stressful life events (SLE) area consider SLEs an environmental risk factor (e.g., Rahe, 1981). Furthermore, the concept of SLE (and the related instruments to measure it) appeared on the scene at about the time when the field of psychosomatic medicine was moving away from an intra-phsychic emphasis and toward an increasing emphasis on social-environmental factors and closer to a social-epidemiological perspective (Kasl, 1977; Lipowski, 1976; Lipowski *et al.*, 1977). Thus, there was a powerful momentum to embrace SLE as a class of risk factors that are apart from characteristics of the person. It is time to examine whether such a view is fully tenable.

Masuda and Holmes (1978) have recently summarized many of their studies and, along the way, have presented mean annual frequencies of life events reported by diverse study groups. Among the groups with very high annual frequencies were heroin addicts (26.3) and alcoholics (19.7); groups with low annual frequencies were medical students (5.0), football players (5.0), medical residents (5.2), and pregnant mothers (5.2). In another report, Goldberg and Comstock (1980) present life event frequencies for some 2780 respondents, comprising two representative samples from Kansas City and Washington County, Maryland. Very strong associations were observed between age and life events reported (and adjusted for other sociodemographic variables): the elderly (65+) reported 11.4 times as often as the young (18–24) no events during one year, while the young were 22.5 times as likely as the elderly to report 5 or more events.

What is the import of such findings? I wish to argue that life events are intimately bound up with a person's lifestyle and reflect, furthermore, the person's stage in the life cycle. It is an intimate and indissoluble concurrent part of being an alcoholic or a heroin addict to experience many life changes. It is part of getting old to experience fewer and fewer life changes. To attempt to argue that SLEs are causally antecedent to heroin use would certainly be foolish, though it is perfectly possible that among heroin addicts SLEs increase the risk of recidivism (Kreuger, 1981). SLEs are not random happenings which follow a Gaussian or a Possion distribution; they are intimately embedded in life cycle and lifestyle dynamics, and they are not part of some separate causal matrix with its own dynamics.

The embeddedness of life events in personal lifestyle characteristics is dramatically illustrated in a longitudinal study of women employees of the Bell Telephone System (Hinkle, 1959): women who were especially 'healthy' (as measured by sickness absences, company dispensary data, and psychiatrists' ratings) were those who were unmarried and were living a routine, dull, withdrawn existence, refusing to get involved with other people. Elsewhere, Hinkle (1974) has emphasized the need to consider the psychological characteristics of people which insulate them against both exposure to events and the impact of such events, if exposed.

Investigators who have worked outside of SLE-disease orientation have had no problem recognizing the difficulty of determining the impact of various events and changes, whenever these are embedded in the lifestyle and life cycle dynamics. For example, the literature on housing moves to the suburbs (Kasl, 1976) suggests that whatever changes do take place after the move, they are appropriately interpreted as 'intended' changes, i.e., the reasons for which the move was made in the first place — increased satisfaction with housing (particularly amount of space), increased social life, and so on. Effects on mental health, family life, or marital happiness are not in evidence. Gans (1963) has particularly forcefully argued for seeing such moves, and any associated changes, as reflecting 'the period of the life cycle, and the opportunities and aspirations associated with class position'. Moves to retirement communities are similarly ambiguous (Kasl and Rosenfield, 1980); for example, changes after the move can be strictly a function of pre-existing goals, plans, and aspirations for a specific retirement setting and the relation of these to the person's assessment of what he/she actually got by moving to that setting.

The viewpoint that many life events are embedded in lifestyle and life cycle dynamics forces us to ask: under what circumstances may 'no change' (no events) be expected to have adverse health consequences? It has been suggested (e.g., Graham, 1974; Neugarten and Datan, 1974) that, from the life cycle perspective, certain events or changes are normative: expected, planned, and desired. When such normal transitions do not take place, this may create as many adaptive demands on the individual as is created (allegedly) by the various stressful life experiences usually enumerated on the various SRE-type instruments. Conversely, what makes some events stressful, Neugarten (1970) suggests, is that they are 'off time' and unanticipated; such events upset the sequence and rhythm of the life cycle. For example, many of the events which elderly individuals experience are expected and 'on time'; this may be one reason why the elderly score SLEs lower on severity or seriousness (Masuda and Holmes, 1978). With respect to bereavement, the elderly face the loss with more cognitive acceptance and the grief is associated with less numbness, denial and guilt (Jacobs and Douglas, 1979). In another area of research, such as occupational mobility, failure to consider job changes (and their absence) in relation to life cycle and career goals has led to inconclusive evidence in which adverse health effects of job changes cannot be detected (e.g., Berkanovic and Korchalk, 1977).

What are the implications of the argument that SLEs are embedded in life cycle and lifestyle dynamics? Certainly, a major consequence is that causal–aetiological interpretations become extremely difficult. In our attempts at causal modelling (e.g., Dohrenwend and Dohrenwend, 1981b; Golden and Dohrenwend, 1981), we will frequently have a difficult time finding the true temporal location of a variable; as a result, more path-analytic models, with quite different causal assumptions, will be compatible with a particular set of findings. Furthermore, it will be much more difficult to know that the relevant other variables have been included in the model. Thus such a model will be guilty of a specification error, a very serious problem for causal modelling (Cook and Campbell, 1979).

Pragmatically, the above argument forces us to look at the events included in the SRE-type instruments with renewed scepticism. Dohrenwend (1974), among others, has noted that the events listed include not only those which are confounded with illness or symptoms (i.e., the dependent variable we wish to study), but also those which appear to be within the subject's control and tend to reflect the subject's superior or inferior functioning. While these ideas have been mostly interpreted as a way of sub-classifying the events (e.g., Fairbank and Hough, 1979), one might well ask whether or not these observations are much more damaging in their implications, demanding that such events be deleted from the various lists.

What would a newly pruned list of SLEs look like if we delete those which are confounded with the outcome and/or are within the subject's control (i.e., embedded in life cycle and lifestyle dynamics)? If one takes the list of 43 events from the Holmes and Rahe (1967) instrument, one finds that the list becomes short indeed: death (of spouse, of close family member, of close friend), and change in health of family member. All the other events are possibly — and often, very likely — within some control of the respondent. A few events, such as retirement, may be outside of the control of many individuals but are certainly fully anticipated and normative in the lifecycle sense. It would thus appear that except for health status changes (including death) happening to significant others, there is little hope we can study the SLE–illness connection without running into serious problems of causal–aetiological interpretation.

Needed Methodological Improvements: Measurement or Research Design?

If our central research goal is to clarify the possible aetiological role of stressful life events in adverse health status changes, then we need to think through the order of methodological priorities which would be most compatible with this goal. I would like to argue that much of the methodological research which has been done in this area is not aetiological research on illness but instrument research on one or another SRE-type instrument; as such, this research has contributed very little to the above central research goal. It has been carried out outside of the health-outcome context, and frequently represents research pursuits along the path of least resistance: cross-sectional paper-and-pencil data are collected on accessible subject populations.

Part of the tremendous growth of the research industry surrounding the SLEs may be attributed to the adoption of a misguided psychometric attitude: the SRE-type instrument looks like a test (e.g., it has individual items); it is used like a test, therefore let's ask the usual psychometric questions. But we are not trying to assess a scientific, dimensional construct, like anxiety or intelligence; we are trying to determine presence or absence of exposure to certain environmental conditions ('experimental treatment') so that we can link it to health outcomes.

When the causal link between exposure to an event (or some collection of events) and illness is far from being an established scientific observation, it is difficult to see how the following types of studies can usefully advance the central research goal: (a) Cross-cultural research on differences in perceptions of life events (e.g., Fairbank and Hough, 1981); the health significance of such differences remains unexamined, though it is possible that SRE will develop into a useful tool for cross-cultural research. Why not do cross-cultural research on health effects of bereavement? (2) Research on various weighting schema in order to arrive at a total score of experienced life events (e.g., Ross and Mirowski, 1979; Shrout, 1981); if a cross-sectional association between reports of SLEs and reports of psychiatric symptoms is ambiguous with respect to causation and can, in fact, represent only the influence of shared response tendencies (social desirability, defensiveness, complaining), then a maximizing weighting schema is just as likely to be maximizing the artifactual influence or response tendency, as increasing the sensitivity to causal effects. In any case, weighting schemata make very little difference; thus the whole effort yields both ambiguous findings and trivial differences. This is not to say, however, that once we have identified events which have strong effects and weak effects, we should not vigorously pursue the question of why the difference. (3) Several authors (e.g., Cleary, 1980; Dohrenwend and Dohrenwend, 1981c; Tausin, 1982) have raised questions regarding the definition of the population (scope) of events which should be included on

SRE-type instruments. In fact, most of the lists different investigators have generated are quite similar (Rahe, 1978) and represent primarily refinements of broad categories of events rather than additional events. The health significance of such minor variations in instruments is not apparent, but is likely to be small at best. It is interesting to note that no one has raised any questions with respect to inclusion–exclusion of events on these instruments from the viewpoint of empirical evidence regarding health impact. For example, there is complete unanimity among reviewers that retirement has no adverse health consequences (e.g., Kasl, 1980; Minkler, 1981; Rowland, 1977; Satariano and Syme, 1981); should we not delete this event from the SRE-type instruments? If not, why not?

In general, there is evidence for increased concern with methodological issues in SLE research. Even 'helpful' checklists have been offered recently (e.g., Cleary, 1980) which laboriously enumerate all the basic research issues, such as sampling, item selection, and appropriate statistics. Yet the fundamental issue of utilizing research designs which permit strong causal inferences is left undiscussed and thus, apparently, unrecognized. It is, of course, also the area in which the investigator is under greatest practical constraints. In the next section, I wish to discuss this issue from the perspective of epidemiology and quasi-experimental field research (e.g. Cook and Campbell, 1979).

A Typology of Longitudinal Research Designs for Stressful Life Experiences

Some of the more visible successes in current epidemiology have come from prospective studies of initially healthy cohorts; viz the studies of coronary heart disease (Pooling Project Research Group, 1978), stroke (Ostfeld, 1980), infectious mononucleosis (Evans, 1978), and so on. This has led to the perception that longitudinal studies are the broad solution to problems of causal inference in stress and disease studies. In this section I wish to examine the extent to which different longitudinal designs help us with the problem of causal inference. I wish to comment on five designs: (1) 'phoney' longitudinal, (2) 'merely' longitudinal ('slice of life'), (3) prospective, (4) doubly prospective, (5) minimal self-selection bias.

The 'phoney' longitudinal study confuses true temporal location of variables with the time at which data on that variable were collected. Typically, one collects self-reports of stressful life events and, at some later time, one collects data on symptoms or physician visits. A correlation between the two variables is interpreted as SLE being the risk factor for later symptoms or illness; but a cross-sectional correlation between the self-same variables would be readily acknowledged as causally ambiguous. However, if the two variables being assessed have a reasonably high temporal stability (or if they are associated with a third variable which is stable, such as defensiveness or complaining), then the longitudinal design does little to reduce the ambiguity of the cross-sectional correlation. A simple reversal in the order of data collection would yield a similar correlation between the two variables but a reversed aetiological interpretation. For example, collecting occupational status data at one point and educational data at a later point will hardly demonstrate the prior aetiological role of occupational status. At a minimum, this design calls for collecting data on both variables at both points in time in order to examine the full set of correlations: cross-sectional, temporal stability, and cross-lagged. However, the cross-lagged panel correlations technique has come under increased criticism (Cook and Campbell, 1979). Another analytical technique is to attempt to predict symptoms at Time 2 from SLEs at Time 1, after symptoms at Time 1 are entered first as a covariate. When this is carried out, one generally finds that the SLEs do not add significantly to one's prediction.

When one collects the full set of variables, one is dealing with what I wish to call the 'slice of life' longitudinal study, characterized by an arbitrary starting point for longitudinal observations. For example, a cross-sectional representative sample of adults in a community is then converted into a longitudinal study by recontacting the respondents at some later point in time. This is a useful design when the follow-up period is a long one, the outcome variable quite different from the predictor variables (such as cancer mortality from some personality trait), and adequate data have been collected on the relevant confounding variables. Thus the Alameda County data have been usefully exploited for looking at the role of social networks in general mortality (Berkman and Syme, 1979) and the Western Electric data were nicely used to examine the role of depression in cancer mortality (Shekelle *et al.*, 1981). On the other hand, when the cohort is picked up at a point when nothing extraordinary is expected to happen, when the period of follow-up is brief, and when the predictors and outcomes are conceptually and methodologically similar, then the expected pay-off from such a study will not be great.

The 'slice of life' longitudinal design may miss the boat (i.e. fail to detect the causal relationships) for two reasons. One is that the cohort may be picked up after the causal dynamics between the risk factor and the health outcome have already played themselves out and we only pick up minor temporal fluctuations in the two variables. For example, taking a sample of blue collar workers (35 years and older) and following them for 5 years in order to discern the mental health impact of a boring, monotonous job may miss the phenomenon altogether: the casualties of inadequate adaptation may have disappeared from observation and the remainder have adapted 'successfully' (e.g., giving up on expecting work to be a meaningful human activity), but the costs of such 'successful' adaptation can no longer be reconstructed through the belated follow-up (Kasl and Cobb, 1982a). Similarly, in a longitudinal study of the elderly, we can only detect predictors of mortality which are influential from the point at which the cohort is brought into the study. If marital status has already had its effect on initial differences in health status (for which we must adjust in our predictor analysis) and has no additional, *de novo* effects during the follow-up, then the effects of marital status are not detected.

A second reason that the 'slice of life' longitudinal design may prove inadequate is that the intervening events between initial and follow-up contacts may be part of a large and rich causal matrix in the manner that SLEs are part of the lifestyle and life cycle dynamics. When that is the case, then we may need a rather intensive schedule of follow-up monitoring in order to detect the true causal sequence. For example, in an analysis of the twenty-year follow-up data on the Midtown Manhattan study (Wexler, 1979), the intervening event of 'retirement' was associated with poorer health in 1974 even after adjusting for health status in 1954. However, this in no way eliminates the possibility that adverse health status changes, say in 1970, were causally antecedent to retirement, say in 1971. Even when the follow-up period is considerably shorter, the same comments apply. In a four-year follow-up of a sample of Chicago residents (Pearlin *et al.*, 1981), the second interview collected data on disruptions in work life: fired, laid off, downgraded, left work because of illness. Collectively, these events were seen as contributing to diminished self-concept (self-esteem, mastery) and higher depression. However, it is again difficult to see how this design and analysis rule out the possiblity that adverse changes in self-esteem and depression took place before the disruptions in work life. The need for careful monitoring of the time sequence of changes, when working with an outcome such as depression, has been emphasized by others (e.g., Tennant *et al.*, 1981).

The scheduling (frequency) of follow-up contacts is important not only for pinning down better the temporal sequence; it also has implications for whether or not one can detect fluctuations and their correlates, whatever the causal interpretation. For example, monthly data collections on psychological symptoms were found to bear a closer association with daily hassles (minor events) than with the usually measured life events (Kanner *et al.*, 1981). Daily collections of data on cigarette consumption were related to daily ratings of stress (Conway *et al.*, 1981); but when cigarette consumption data cover a period of months, very little fluctuation of consumption in relation to stress may be observed (Kasl and Cobb, 1980). In general, it is prudent to assume that many of our independent and dependent variables may be sensitive only when covering a specific span of time, and that covariation may not be detected when one is working outside of such time spans.

The temporal location of a specific event in relation to the initial and follow-up data collection may also affect our ability to detect and interpret changes. Consider self-esteem in relation to separation or divorce. If one assumes that self-esteem begins to decline some time prior to the actual date of the event and recovers gradually, then individuals whose separation/divorce took place shortly after the first interview should show an increase in self-esteem over the study period, while those whose separation/divorce took place close to the second interview, should show a decline. However, the usual analysis is to compare temporal trends for all cases (separation/divorce in the intervening period) versus all controls. But this will average out heterogeneous trends among cases, and case-control differences will show little. And if the decline and recovery trends in self-esteem in relation to the date of the event are highly idiosyncratic, then our ability to analyse and make sense of the temporal trends over the study period are further reduced. These comments, of course, are intended to be generic for many events and many dependent variables.

The next design is the classical prospective cohort study in epidemiology. It differs from the 'slice of life' design in two meaningful ways: only subjects free of the target disease are brought into the study, and the age range of the cohort is (hopefully) optimal for detecting the transition from risk factor to overt disease. Unfortunately, there are several reasons why the classical prospective study design would prove inadequate in life events–illness studies. For one, the prospective incidence study is dependent on the presence of one or more clinical features of the disease, such as: (a) dramatic sudden onset (e.g., an attack of gout) which can yield adequate recall; (b) severity of episode which nearly always leads to some medical attention (e.g., an MI); (c) an irreversible diagnostic sign (e.g., characteristic EKG pattern after a 'silent' MI). On the other hand, intermittent conditions with gradual onset and full remission of signs and symptoms, are more difficult to study.

However, there are more fundamental issues. When we assess serum cholesterol at the start of our prospective study of CHD, we do not worry about: (a) the issue of self-selection into initially high vs. low risk factor status, and (b) the reactive effects of high cholesterol levels. However, when we are examining stressful life events as a possible risk factor, we are eminently concerned with both issues. As I have argued already, life events do not necessarily represent random environmental exposure; they are embedded in a causal matrix which makes the temporal location of such events more ambiguous and which substantially increases the likelihood of spurious associations between life events and some outcomes. Furthermore, life events are hardly 'silent' risk factors the way high blood pressure or high cholesterol are. Individuals respond to life events, they cope and they adapt (or fail to adapt), and thus the meaning of the initial assessment of the risk factor, life events, can be drastically altered by these later processes.

The notion of a doubly prospective study is the notion of picking up a cohort before onset of disease and before onset of risk factors as well. For stressful life events research, this implies obtaining initial or baseline data before the event or events have taken place. This is a superficially attractive idea but the design does not really get rid of the entire problem of self-selection into different events and the problem of confounded causal relationships, because of the embeddedness of various life events in the lifestyle–life cycle matrix. One can study retirement prospectively, but when is the proper time to start collecting baseline data (Kasl, 1980)? One could study divorce prospectively, but any particular starting time is just an earlier stage in the development of the marriage. The problems of studying other voluntary changes such as residential moves have already been discussed. It is thus apparent that the idea of a doubly prospective study is attractive only when it applies to life events over which the person has little control; as noted earlier, there are very few such events, indeed. The alternative of getting respondents to evaluate subjectively and after-the-fact whether or not an event was under their control — and then studying only the impact of those events designated as beyond control — is rather unpalatable. It is hard to imagine what it would mean when a respondent indicates that a marital separation was beyond his/her control; other judgements of beyond control, such as for 'being fired', would at best be suspect.

The idea of doubly prospective design is also unattractive if it were to imply that we should start the cohort study only with those respondents who report zero events on an SRE-type instrument. Aside from the possible problems of statistical regression created by such a selection, it is doubtful that such a sample of respondents would have a useful or determinable representativeness.

The Opportunistic Study of Single Events or Natural Clusters of Events

The above considerations point to the considerable difficulty of applying a simple epidemiological model to the study of life events and illness by using the SRE-type instrument to measure the risk factor and by studying an unselected population sample. 'Inferring cause from passive observation' (a chapter title in the excellent book by Cook and Campbell, 1979, on quasi-experimentation) is just too difficult when we try at the same time to retain the broadest representativeness of our study population and work with an instrument, like the SRE, which (aside from its evident methodological limitations) ambitiously tries to characterize a large chunk of a person's social situation and experience.

The alternative strategy of studying single events (or naturally occurring clusters of events) has much to recommend it. Single, non-trivial events are difficult enough to study, but only by studying them does one learn of their complexity. For example, several authors (Hull, 1979; McKinley, 1975; Prior, 1977; Wessen, 1971) have commented on and analysed the complex phenomenon of migration: the point in time in which the person participates in the process; the demographic and socio-psychological characteristics of the migrants due to self-selection and the changes in these at different stages of the migration process; the nature of the environmental change; the nature of the adaptation and assimilation process; the role of diet, physical activity, health habits, and utilization of health services; and so on. To embed migration in a large list of events would be to give up any chances of studying this event effectively. Job loss is another event which is enormously complex (Cobb and Kasl, 1977; Kasl, 1979, 1982b; Kasl and Cobb, 1982b), and even a relatively clean 'natural experiment' — a permanent plant shut-down in which everyone loses their job through no fault of their own and where the cohort is picked up from before the plant closes — does not permit a full ascertainment of the causal dynamics.

Even rather specific and apparently clear-cut events may have hidden complexities. For example, involuntary residential moves of institutionalized geriatric populations were found associated with increased mortality in studies before 1970, but not since then (Dube, 1982,; Kasl and Rosenfield, 1980). A very likely possibility is that the early studies influenced the way in which the latter moves were handled (individualized attention, casework service, psychological support); this changed the phenomenon sufficiently so that the negative health impact was prevented. Involuntary residential moves of the elderly within the community have also undergone secular changes, and the phenomenon is quite different from the heyday of urban renewal activity (Kasl and Rosenfield, 1980).

For many disease outcomes, a great deal of detail of description of the stressful experience may be needed before a causal relationship is manifest; such detail is, of course, facilitated by the intensive study of single events or event clusters. For example, recent reviews of the connection between stress and heightened susceptibility or immunosuppression (e.g., Ader, 1981; Fox, 1981; Rogers *et al.*, 1979; Sklar and Anisman, 1981) are in complete agreement on the conclusion that 'stress' may enhance as well as decrease susceptibility to disease; the immune system is much too complex a network, and a variety of factors in the host, in the challenge to be the host, and in the chronicity and intensity of the challenge must also be considered.

The strategy of studying single events or event clusters is not primarily a strategy of retreat, a decision to study a smaller chunk of the phenonmenon. Opportunities for studying 'natural experiments' (significant social events which are predictable because of social planning or social dynamics and which can be studied in their natural setting with sufficient scientific rigour) are overwhelmingly single events or event clusters: the closing of a plant, the automation of a department, the arrival of new industry in a rural area, and so on. Such events allow us to minimize self-selection problems and to study them more convincingly in the spirit of environmental influences impinging on the person from the 'outside'.

A number of writers (e.g., Cohen, 1980; Dohrenwend and Dohrenwend, 1978; Helzer, 1981; Jenkins, 1979; Mechanic, 1974) have emphasized the need to study the psychosocial modifiers of the response to stress and to understand how life events may interact with various social-psychological and intrapsychic variables; the controllability and predictability of life events have been especially singled out as important qualities which can modify effects. When we are dealing with unselected populations and long lists of events, we are forced to depend on the respondent's own perceptions of the events. However, such subjective, retrospective evaluations are very likely to be seriously contaminated with many outcomes of interest. And respondent's *a priori* preconceptions about possible future events, such as with respect of perceptions of control, are not necessarily related to their perceptions when the events do happen (Dohrenwend and Martin, 1979). However, when we are studying single events in a setting of a 'natural experiment' we have an opportunity to collect additional information about the event and about its social setting from institutional records, the planners involved in the event, and selected significant others. Thus the possibly contaminated perceptions of our respondents are not the only source of our data about the event.

One of the modifiers of the impact of a particular event may, in fact, be the broader context of other stressful events experienced by the individual. For example, in the already mentioned study of plant closing (Cobb and Kasl, 1977) it was deemed necessary to monitor other stressful life events with an SRE-type instrument in order to determine whether the job loss precipitated other life changes or if the impact was restricted only to the work role. A particularly interesting interaction was reported by Ruch *et al.* (1980) in their study of rape impact: while severe life crises were not found to facilitate coping with rape, individuals with no recent events had a somewhat worse outcome than persons reporting recent minor events. (Of course, it is not clear whether in focusing on respondents with no events we are selecting out defensive individuals, or those with a particular lifestyle, or perhaps just those who 'happen' not to have experienced any events.) And the whole literature on social factors in the health of the elderly calls for the study of specific events, frequent among the elderly, in relation to (among others) previous events experienced, in order to see if previous events increase or reduce the vulnerability of the elderly to events in old age (Kasl and Berkman, 1981). In short, the strategy of studying single events or event clusters need not mean a complete abandonment of the SRE-type instrument; rather, it represents a refocusing of research design and research strategy.

Salvaging Some Respectability for Cross-sectional and Case-Control Studies

The previous two sections of this chapter should not be interpreted as a call for the total abandonment of retrospective studies in SLE research. Certainly, for events and/or outcomes when there is no accumulated research evidence, a retrospective study design appears to be a reasonable, cost-efficient starting point. It may be useful to suggest very briefly other research topics where retrospective study designs can make their contribution: (1) Cross-cultural or international studies may yield suggestive differences with weak designs. For example, Orth-Gomer (1979) carried out a case-control study of men in New York and Stockholm with and without ischemic heart disease. The Swedish man ascribed stress mainly to the job situation, while American men reported stress caused by family conflict, but there were no differences in overall quantity of stress. While this could reflect only cross-cultural differences in the attribution process, differential aetiological processes may also be involved. (2) Studies which seek to understand the processes of what makes life events stressful may have to begin with a retrospective design. For example, Totman (1979), in his study of MI patients and controls, found that the MI patients reported for the pre-morbid year a significantly greater reduction in socializing as a result of life events. This agrees rather well with the laboratory research results of a greater insensitivity towards others after stressful exposure (Cohen, 1980), and may give us useful leads about the complex role of social support in the stress–disease association. (3) If we can assume that the same potential biases in recall and reporting apply to different patient groups, then a retrospective study of differences between patient groups may prove useful. For example, Leavitt *et al.*, (1979) compared reports of SLEs for different groups of patients with low back pain, differentiated only later by clincial evaluation for presence of definite organic disease. Paykel *et al.* (1975) compared suicide attempters with patients seeking treatment for depression (and community controls). The fact that attempters tended to have more 'entrance' events (vs. 'exits' or social losses), even though these did not differentiate depressives from community controls, suggests that social processes leading to a suicide attempt may be different from those leading to seeking help for depression. (4) The first step in exploring the promise of some variable thought to moderate the effects of SLE may reasonably be a retrospective study. The role of Type A Behaviour (Suls *et al.*, 1979) and sensation seeking (Cooley and Kessey, 1981) was examined in this preliminary fashion. Of course, if the measurement of the putative moderator variable is influenced by the same traits or processes which affect the measurement of the SLEs and/or the outcome, then the promise of this moderator variable will have been falsely demonstrated.

Epilogue

Significant social problems come in uncomfortably large clusters and packages and the scientist is stymied in his efforts to unravel these and label some 'causes' and other 'effects'. For example, the many sides of poverty are seen in the co-existence or co-occurrence of a large number of interrelated problems: physical illness, mental illness, low income, unemployment, social disorganization, racial discrimination, broken families, poor housing, slum location, crime and delinquency, alcoholism and drug abuse, and so on. A scientist who boldly steps in and imposes causal arrows on these variables had better have a strong research design to back him up.

In the area of stressful life experiences and disease, many investigators have assumed that SLEs are a relatively independent environmental influence which will act like a string at which we can pull and the whole package will unravel and reveal the hidden causal dynamics. In this chapter I have tried to suggest that this is not a fully justifiable attitude, particularly when wedded to the methodology of using a summative list of events to describe the environmental condition and working with unselected population samples. Different research strategies were discussed and the usefulness of the single event strategy in a 'natural experiment' setting was defended.

References

Ader, R. (1981) Behavioral influences on immune responses. In Weiss, S. M., Herd, J. A., and Fox, B. H. (Eds), *Perspectives on Behavioral Medicine*. New York: Academic Press, 163–82.

Berkanovic, E., and Korchalk, P. C. (1977) Occupational mobility and health. In Kasl, S. V., and Reichsman, F. (Eds), *Advances in Psychosomatic Medicine*, Vol. 9. Basel: Karger, 132–9.

Berkman, L. F., and Syme, S. L. (1979) Social networks, host resistance, and mortality: A nine-year follow-up study of Alameda County residents. *Amer. J. Epidemiol.*, **109**, 186–204.

Brand, R. J., Rosenman, R. H., Sholtz, R. J., and Friedman, M. (1976) Multivariate prediction of coronary heart disease in the Western Collaborative Group Study compared to the findings of the Framingham Study. *Circul.* **53**, 348–55.

Cleary, P. J. (1980) A checklist for life event research. *J. Psychosom. Res.*, **24**, 199–207.

Cobb, S., and Kasl, S. V. (1977) Termination: The Consequences of Job Loss. Washington, D.C.: USDHEW, PHS, CDC, NIOSH, HEW Publication No. (NIOSH) 76–1261.

Cohen, S. (1980) After-effects of stress on human performance and social behaviour: A review of research and theory. *Psychol. Bull.*, **88**, 82–108.

Conway, T. L., Vickers, R. R., Jr., Ward, H. W., and Rahe, R. H. (1981) Occupational stress and variation in cigarette, coffee, and alcohol consumption. *J. Hlth. Soc. Behav.*, **22**, 155–65.

Cook, T. D., and Campbell, D. T. (1979) *Quasi-Experimentation: Design and Analysis Issues for Field Settings*. Chicago: Rand McNally.

Cooley, E. J., and Kessey, J. C. (1981) Moderator variables in life stress and illness relationships. *J. Hum. Stress*, **7**(3), 35–40.

Crook, T., and Eliot, J. (1980) Parental death during childhood and adult depression: A critical review of the literature. *Psychol. Bull.*, **87**, 252–9.

Dohrenwend, B. P. (1974) Problems in defining and sampling the relevant population of stressful life events. In Dohrenwend, B. S., and Dohrenwend, B. P., *Stressful Life Events: Their Nature and Effects*. New York: Wiley, 275–310.

Dohrenwend, B. P., and Dohrenwend, B. S. (1981b) Socioenvironmental factors, stress, and psychopathology. *Amer. J. Community Psychol.*, **9**, 128–59.

Dohrenwend, B. S., and Dohrenwend, B. P. (Eds) (1974) *Stressful Life Events*. New York: Wiley.

Dohrenwend, B. S., and Dohrenwend, B. P. (1978) Some issues in research on stressful life events. *J. Nerv. Ment. Dis.*, **166**, 7–15.

Dohrenwend, B. S., and Dohrenwend, B. P. (Eds) (1981a) *Stressful Life Events and Their Contexts*. Ne York: Prodist.

Dohrenwend, B. S., and Dohrenwend, B. P. (1981c) Life stress and illness; formulation of the issues. In Dohrenwend, B. S. and Dohrenwend, B. P. (Eds), *Stressful Life Events and Their Contexts*. New York: Prodist, 1–27.

Dohrenwend, B. S., Krasnoff, L., Askenasy, A. R., and Dohrenwend, B. P. (1978) Exemplification of a method for scaling life events: the PERI life events scale. *J. Hlth. Soc. Behav.*, **19**, 205–29.

Dohrenwend, B. S., and Martin, J. L. (1979) Personal versus situational determination of anticipation and control of the occurrence of stressful life events. *Amer. J. Community Psychol.* **7**, 453–68.

Dube, A. H. (1982) The impact of moving a geriatric population: mortality and emotional aspects. *J. Chron. Dis.*, **35**, 61–4.

Elesh, D., and Lefcowitz, M. J. (1977) The effects of the New Jersey–Pennsylvania negative income tax experience on health and health care utilization. *J. Health Soc. Behav.*, **18**, 391–405.

Evans, A. S. (1978) Infectious mononucleosis and related syndromes. *Amer, J. Med. Sci.*, **276**, 325–39.

Fairbank, D. T., and Hough, R. L. (1979) Life event classifications and the event–illness relationship. *J. Hum. Stress*, **5**(3), 41–7.

Fairbank, D. T., and Hough, R. L. (1981) Cross-cultural differences in perceptions of life events. In Dohrenwend, B. S., und Dohenwend, B. P. (Eds), *Stressful Life Events and Their Contexts*. New York: Prodist, 63–84.

Fenwick, R., and Barresi, C. M. (1981) Health consequences of marital-status change among the elderly: A comparison of cross-sectional and longitudinal analyses. *J. Hlth. & Soc. Behav.*, **22**, 106–16.

Fox, B. H. (1981) Psychosocial factors and the immune system in human cancer. In Ader, R. (Ed.) *Psychoneuroimmunology*. New York: Academic Press.

Gans, H. J. (1963) Effects of the move from city to suburb. In Duhl, L. G., (Ed.), *The Uban Condition*. New York: Basic Books, 184–98.

Goldberg, E. L., and Comstock, G. W. (1976) Life events and subsequent illness. *Amer. J. Epidemiol.*, **104**, 146–58.

Goldberg, E. L., and Comstock, G. W. (1980) Epidemiology of life events: frequency in general populations. *Amer. J. Epidemiol.*, **111**, 736–52.

Golden, R. R., and Dohrenwend, B. S. (1981) A path analytic method for testing causal hypotheses about the life stress process. In Dohrenwend, B. S., and Dohrenwend, B. P. (Eds), *Stressful Life Events and Their Contexts*. New York: Prodist, 258–78.

Graham, S. (1974) The sociological approach to epidemiology. *Amer. J. Pub. Hlth.*, **64**, 1046–9.

Hawkins, N. G., Davies, R., and Holmes, T. H. (1957) Evidence of psychosocial factors in the development of pulmonary tuberculosis. *Amer. Rev. Tuberc. Pulmon. Dis.*, **75**, 768–80.

Helsing, K. J., and Szklo, M (1981) Mortality after bereavement. *Amer. J. Epidemiol.*, **114**, 41–52.

Helzer, J. E. (1981) Methodological issues in the interpretations of the consequences of extreme situations. In Dohrenwend, B. S., and Dohrenwend, B. P. (Eds), *Stressful Events and Their Contexts*. New York: Prodist, 108–29.

Heyman, D. K., and Giaturco, D. T. (1973) Long-term adaptation by the elderly to bereavement. *J. Gerontol.,* **28**, 359–62.

Hinkle, L. E., Jr. (1959) Physical health, mental health, and the social environment: Some characteristics of healthy and unhealthy people. In Ojeman, R. G. (Ed.), *Recent Contributions of Biological and Psychosocial Investigations to Preventive Psychiatry*. Iowa City: State University of Iowa, 80–103.

Hinkle, L. E., Jr. (1974) The effect of exposure to culture change, social change, and changes in interpersonal relationships on health. In Dohrenwend, B. S., and Dohrenwend, B. O. (Eds), *Stressful Life Events: Their Nature and Effects*. New York: Wiley, 9–44.

Holmes, T. H., and Rahe, R. H. (1967) The social readjustment rating scale. *J. Psychosom. Res.*, **11**, 213–18.

Horowitz, M., Schaefer, C., Hiroto, D., Wilner, N., and Levin, B. (1977) Life event questionnaires for measuring presumptive stress. *Psychosom. Med.*, **39**, 413–31.

Hudgens, R. W. (1974) Personal catastrophe and depression: A consideration of the subject with respect of medically ill adolescents, and a requiem for retrospective life-event studies. In Dohrenwend, B. S., and Dohrenwend, B. P. (Eds), *Stressful Life Events: Their Nature and Effects*. New York: Wiley, 119–34.

Hull, D. (1979) Migration, adaptation, and illness: A review. *Soc. Sci. & Med.*, **13**(A), 25–36.

Hurst, M. W., Jenkins, C. D., and Rose, R. M. (1976) The relation of psychological stress to onset of medical illness. *Ann. Rev. Med.*, **27**, 301–12.

Hurst, M. W., Jenkins, C. D., and Rose, R. M. (1978) The assessment of life change stress: A comparative and methodological inquiry. *Psychosom. Med.*, **40**, 126–41.

Jacobs, S., and Douglas, L. (1979) Grief: A mediating process between loss and illness. *Comprehens. Psychiat.*, **20**, 165–74.

Jacobs, S., and Ostfeld, A. M. (1977) An epidemiological review of mortality of bereavement. *Psychosom Med.*, **39**, 344–57.

Jenkins, C. D. (1976) Recent evidence supporting psychologic and social risk factors for coronary disease. *New Engl. J. Med.*, **294**, 987–94, and 1033–38.

Jenkins, C. D. (1979) Psychosocial modifiers of response to stress. *J. Hum. Stress*, **5** (4), 3–15.

Kanner, A. D., Coyne, J. C., Schaefer, C., and Lazarus, R. S. (1981) Comparison of two modes of stress measurement: daily hassles and uplifts versus major life events. *J. Behav. Med.*, **4**, 1–39.

Kasl, S. V. (1976) Effects of housing on mental and physical health. In *Housing in the Seventies Working Papers 1*. Washington, D. C.: U.S. Department of Housing and Urban Development, 286–304.

Kasl, S. V. (1977) Contributions of social epidemiology to studies in psychosomatic medicine. In Kasl, S. V., and Reichsman, F. (Eds), *Advances in Psychosomatic Medicine*, Vol. 9. Basel: Kaager, 160–223.

Kasl, S. V. (1979) Changes in mental health status associated with job loss and retirement. In Barrett, J. E. (Ed.), *Stress and Mental Disorders*. New York: Raven Press, 179–200.

Kasl, S. V. (1980) The impact of retirement. In Cooper, C. L., and Payne, R. (Eds), *Current Concerns in Occupational Stress*. Chichester: J. Wiley, 137–86.

Kasl, S. V. (1981) The effect of stress and other psychosocial factors in the development of coronary heart disease. *Washington Pub. Hlth.*, **2**(2), 18–21.

Kasl, S. V. (1982a) Social and psychological factors affecting the course of disease: An epidemiological perspective. In Mechanic, D. (Ed.), *Handbook of Health, Health Care, and the Health Profession*. New York: Free Press (in press).

Kasl, S. V. (1982b) Strategies of research on economic instability and health. *Psychol. Med.*, **12** (in press).

Kasl, S. V., and Berkman, L. F. (1981) Some psychosocial influences on the health status of the elderly: The perspective of social epidemiology. In McGaugh, J. L., and Kiesler, S. B. (Eds), *Aging: Biology and Behaviour*. New York: Academic Press, 345–85.

Kasl, S. V., and Cobb, S. (1980) The experience of losing a job: Some effects on cardiovascular functioning. *Psychother. Psychosom.*, **34**, 88–109.

Kasl, S. V., and Cobb, S. (1982a) Psychological and social stresses in the work place. In Levy, B. S., and Wegman, D. H. (Eds), *Occupational Health: Recognizing and Preventing Work-Related Disease*. Boston: Little, Brown, and Co. (in press).

Kasl, S. V., and Cobb, S. (1982b) Variability of stress effects among men experiencing job loss. In Goldberger, L., and Breznitz, S. (Eds.), *Handbook of Stress*. New York: The Free Press (in press).

Kasl, S. V., Evans, A. S., and Niederman, J. C. (1979) Psychosocial risk factors in the development of infectious mononucleosis. *Psychosom. Med.*, **41**, 445–66.

Kasl, S. V., and Rosenfield, S. (1980) The residential environment and its impact on the mental health of the aged. In Birren, J. E., and Sloane, R. B. (Eds), *Handbook of Mental Health and Aging*. Englewood Cliffs, N. J.: Prentice Hall, Inc., 468–98.

Kittel, F., Kornitzer, M., and Dramaix, M. (1980) Coronary heart disease and job stress in two cohorts of bank clerks. *Psychother. Psychosom.*, **34**, 110–23.

Krueger, D. W. (1981) Stressful life events and the return to heroin use. *J. Hum. Stress*, **7**(2), 3–8.

Leavitt, F., Garron, D. C., and Bielauskas, L. A. (1979) Stressing life events and the experience of low back pain. *J. Psychosom. Res.*, **23**, 49–55.

Lipowski, Z. J. (1976) Psychosomatic medicine: an overview. In Hill, O. (Ed.), *Modern Trends in Psychosomatic Medicine*, Vol. 3. London: Butterworths, 1–20.

Lipowski, Z. J., Lipsitt, D. R., and Whybrow, P. C. (Eds) (1977) *Psychosomatic Medicine: Current Trends and Clincal Applications*. New York: Oxford University Press.

McGill, H. C., Jr., and Stern, M. P. (1979) Sex and atherosclerosis. In Paoletti, R., and Gotto, A. M., Jr. (Eds), *Atherosclerosis Reviews*, Vol. 4. New York: Raven Press, 157–242.

McKinley, J. B. (1975) Some issues associated with migration, health status, and the use of health services. *J. Chron. Dis..*, **28**, 579–92.

Marmot, M. G., Rose, G., Shipley, M., and Hamilton, P. J. J. (1978) Employment grade and coronary heart disease in British civil servants. *J. Epid. & Community Hlth.*, **32**, 244–9.

Masuda, M., and Holmes, T. H. (1978) Life events: perceptions and frequencies. *Psychosom. Med.*, **40**, 236–69.

Mechanic, D. (1974) Discussion of research programs on relations between stressful life events and episodes of physical illness. In Dohrenwend, B. S., and Dohrenwend, B. P. (Eds), *Stressful Life Events: Their Nature and Effects*. New York: Wiley, 87–97.

Minkler, M. (1981) Research on the health effects of retirement: An uncertain legacy. *J. Hlth. Soc. Behav.*, **22**, 117–30.

Nuegarten, B. L. (1970) Adaptation and the life cycle. *J. Geriat. Psychiat.*, **4**, 71–100.

Neugarten, B. L., and Datan, N. (1974) The middle years. In Arieti, S. (Ed.), *American Handbook of Psychiatry*, Vol. 1. New York: Basic Books, 592–608.

Orth-Gomer, K. (1979) Ischemic heart disease and psychological stress in Stockholm and New York. *J. Psychosom. Res.*, **23**, 165–73.

Ostfeld, A. M. (1980) A review of stroke epidemiology. *Epidemiologic Reviews*, **2**, 136–52.

Paykel, E. S., Myers, J. K., Dienelt, M. N., Klerman, G. L., Lindenthal, J. J., and Pepper, M. P. (1969) Life events and depression: A controlled study. *Arch. Gen. Psychiat.*, **21**, 753–60.

Paykel, E. S., Prusoff, B. A., and Myers, J. K. (1975) Suicide attempts and recent life events. *Arch. Gen. Psychiat.*, **32**, 327–33.

Paykel, E. S., Prusoff, B. A., and Uhlenhuth, E. H. (1971) Scaling of life events. *Arch. Gen. Psychiat.*, **25**, 340–7.

Pearlin, L. I., Lieberman, M. A., Menaghan, E. G., and Mullan, J. T. (1981) The stress process. *J. Hlth. Soc. Behav.*, **22**, 337–56.

Pooling Project Research Group (1978) Relationship of blood pressure, serum cholesterol, smoking habit, relative weight and ECG abnormalities to incidence of major coronary events. Final report of the pooling project. *J. Chron. Dis.*, **31**, 201–306.

Prior, I. (1977) Migration and physical illness. In Kasl, S. V., and Reichsman, F. (Eds), *Advances in Psychosomatic Medicine*, Vol. 9. Basel: Karger, 105–31.

Rabkin, J. G. (1980) Stressful life events and schizophrenia: A review of the research literature. *Psychol. Bull.*, **87**, 408–25.

Rahe, R. H. (1978) Life change measurement clarification. *Psychosom. Med.*, **40**, 95–8.

Rahe, R. H. (1981) Developments in life change measurement: Subjective life change unit scaling. In Dohrenwend, B. S., and Dohrenwend, B. P. (Eds), *Stressful Life Events and Their Contexts*. New York: Prodist, 48–62.

Rogers, M. P., Dubey, D., and Reich, P. (1979) The influence of the psyche and the brain on immunity and disease susceptibility: A critic review. *Psychosomatic Medicine*, **41**, 147–64.

Ross, C. E., and Mirowski, J., II. (1979) A comparison of life-event-weighting schemes: Change, undesirability, and effect-proportional indices. *J. Hlth. Soc. Behav.*, **20**, 166–77.

Rowland, K. F. (1977) Environmental events predicting death for the elderly. *Psychol. Bull.*, **84**, 349–72.

Ruch, L. D., Chandler, S. M., and Harter, R. A. (1980) Life change and rape impact. *J. Hlth. Soc. Behav.*, **21**, 248–60.

Rundall, T. G. (1978) Life change and recovery from surgery. *J. Hlth. & Soc. Behav.*, **19**, 418–27.

Russek, H. I. (1962) Emotional stress and coronary heart disease in American physicians, dentists, and lawyers. *Amer. J. Med. Sci.*, **243**, 716–25.

Russek, H. I. (1965) Stress, tobacco, and coronary disease in North American professional groups. *J.A.M.A.*, **192**, 189–94.

Satariano, W. A., and Syme, S. L. (1981) Life changes and disease in elderly populations. In McGaugh, J. L., and Kiesler, S. B. (Eds), *Aging: Biology and Behavior*. New York: Academic Press, 311–27.

Shekelle, R. B., and Lin, S. C. (1978) Public beliefs about causes and prevention of heart attacks. *J.A.M.A.*, **240**, 756–8.

Shekelle, R. B., Raynor, W. J., Ostfeld, A. M., Garron, D. C., Bielanskas, L. A.,

Lin, S. C., Maliza, C., and Paul, O. (1981) Psychological depression and 17-year risk of death from cancer. *Psychosom. Med.*, **43**, 117–25.

Shrout, P. E. (1981) Scaling of stressful life events. In Dohrenwend, B. S., and Dohrenwend, B. P. (Eds), *Stressful Life Events and Their Contexts*. New York: Prodist, 29–47.

Sklar, L. S., and Anisman, H. (1981) Stress and cancer. *Psychol. Bull.*, **89**, 369–406.

Suls, J., Gastorf, J. W., and Witenberg, S. H. (1979) Life events, psychological distress, and the Type A Coronary-Prone Behavior Pattern. *J. Psychosom. Res.*, **23**, 315–19.

Susser, M. (1981a) The epidemiology of life stress. *Psychol. Med.*, **11**, 1–8.

Susser, M. (1981b) Widowhood: A situational life stress or a stressful life event. *Amer. J. Pub. Hlth.*, **71**, 793–5.

Talbott, E., Kuller, L. H., Perper, J., and Murphy, P. A. (1981) Sudden unexpected death in women: Biologic and psychosocial origins. *Amer. J. Epidemiol.*, **114**, 671–82.

Tausig, M. (1982) Measuring life events. *J. Hlth. Soc. Behav.*, **23**, 52–64.

Tennant, C., Bebbington, P., and Hurry, J. (1980) Parental death in childhood and risk of adult depressive disorders: A review. *Psychol. Med.*, **10**, 289–99.

Tennant, C., Bebbington, P., and Hurry, J. (1981) The role of life events in depressive illness: is there a substantial causal relation. *Psychol. Med.*, **11**, 379–89.

Totman, R. (1979) What makes life events stressful? A retrospective study of patients who have suffered a first myocardial infarction. *J. Psychosom. Res.*, **23**, 193–201.

Wershaw, H. J., and Reinhart, G. (1974) Life change and hospitalization — A heretical view. *J. Psychosom. Res.*, **18**, 393–401.

Wessen, A. F. (1971) The role of migrant studies in epidemiological research. *Israel J. Med. Scis.*, **7** 1584–91.

Wexler, L. M. (1979) *Long-Range Predictors of Change and Stability in Adult Mental Health*. New Haven: Yale University Department of Epidemiology and Public Health (unpublished doctoral dissertation).

Stress Research
Edited by Cary L. Cooper
© 1983, John Wiley & Sons, Ltd.

Chapter 5
Problem Areas for Future Stress Research: Cancer and Working Women

Cary L. Cooper
Professor of Organizational Psychology, Department of Management Sciences,
University of Manchester Institute of Science and Technology, UK

Over the last couple of decades, there has been an enormous amount of attention devoted to the field of occupational and life stress as it relates to coronary heart disease (Cooper and Marshall, 1976; Glass, 1977; Greenberg, 1980; Cooper, 1981), particularly among male workers. There have been large-scale prospective national studies, such as the Western Collaborative (Rosenman, Friedman, and Jenkins, 1967) and the Framingham studies (Haynes, Feinleib, and Kannel, 1980), which have enhanced our understanding of the stressors and processes of coronary heart disease. A prominent feature of their effort has been a concentration on what has been termed in medical circles as the 'psychosocial' factors, that is, the personality and social-psychological precursors to heart disease. While research into coronary heart disease and stress has been growing, developing and bearing valuable information, the same cannot be said of other potentially stress-related illnesses, particularly cancer. In addition, even the work on coronary heart disease has focused primarily on men, so another important area of future research should include greater attention to the problems of working women, who are becoming a much larger element of the workforce in almost all developed countries.

The author felt, therefore, that it might be useful here to highlight two potential fields of study, which are in their infancy in terms of stress research, but which are likely to or should occupy a greater share of our attention in the future: the relationship between psychosocial stress and cancer (and the methodological problems), and the pressures of working women (and what can be done about them).

Stress and Cancer

The relationship of psychological factors to cancer

It was in the late nineteenth century that attention was first drawn to the possible link of stress and cancer by Herbert Snow (1893) in his book *Cancer and the Cancer Process*:

> We are logically impelled to inquire if the great majority of cases of cancer may not own a neurotic origin. . .? We find that a number of instances in which malignant disease of the breast and uterus follows immediately antecedent emotion of a depressing character is too large to be set down to chance, or to that general liability to the buffets of ill fortune which the cancer patient, in their passage through life, share with most other people not so afflicted.

Throughout the early part of the twentieth century, further suggestions have been made about the relationship between psychosocial factors and cancer, culminating in a book by Evans (1926) on *A Psychological Study of Cancer*, in which she suggested that one of the leading causes of cancer was the loss of a love object or an important emotional relationship. Her analysis of cancer patients led her to believe that some people experiencing grief directed their psychic energy inward, against their own natural body defences.

There have been a number of explanations of just how stress may cause disease. Fox (1978), for example, suggests that there are two primary cancer-causing mechanisms: (1) 'carcinogenesis, the production of cancer by an agent or mechanism overcoming existing resistance of the body', and (2) 'lowered resistance to cancer, which permits a potential carcinogen normally insufficient to produce cancer to do so' (e.g. weakened emotional state). This latter mechanism involves the immunosuppression system of the body, with an 'immune deficient' individual *at risk* to one form of cancer or another, depending on the vulnerability of particular organs.

Selye (1979), on the other hand, suggests that all organisms go through a 'general adaptation syndrome', which passes through three stages:

1. *Alarm reaction*, which is comprised of a *shock phase* ('the initial and immediate reaction to a noxious agent') and a *countershock phase* ('a mobilization of defences phase in which the adrenal cortex becomes further enlarged and secretes more corticoid hormones').
2. *Stage of resistance*, which involves adapting to the stressor stimulus, but decreasing one's ability to cope with subsequent stimuli.
3. *Stage of exhaustion*, which follows a period of prolonged and severe adaptation.

Selye goes on to say that the hormonal attack (particularly adrenocortico-trophic hormone or ACTH) on the body, is the ultimate cancer-producing weapon if it is activated at a frequent, continuous and high level.

Seyle believes that stress plays some role in the development of all diseases:

> these effects may be curative (as illustrated by various forms of externally-induced stress such as shock therapy, physical therapy, and occupational therapy) or damaging, depending on whether the biochemical reactions characteristic of stress (e.g. stress hormones or nervous reactions to stress) combat or accentuate the trouble.

Whereas Fox (1978) and Selye (1979) emphasize the physiological or bodily reactions and processes of stress, Haney (1977), Kissen (1969), and others have concentrated on the psychological processes that may lead to cancer. Kissen has argued that adverse life events and loss of a love object can lead to cancer by the psychological mechanisms of 'despair, depression and hopelessness'. He suggests:

> adverse life situations in an individual with poor emotional outlets, and therefore, with diminished ability to effectively sublimate or dissipate an emotional situation, are likely to result in such effects as depression, despair and hopelessness. It is also possible that adverse life situations may directly precipitate such effects whatever the personality, but it must be conceded that their manifestation is more likely in those with poor emotional outlets.

Haney (1977) argues that personality predispositions may not be directly linked to cancer, but will help to determine 'which psychic and somatic insults to which the individual will be exposed and the meaning of these exposures will have for the individual'. There is likely to be a psycho-carcinogenic process in operation, which works in such a way that the stressor and bodily predispositions interact and co-vary in the direction of an ultimate carcinoma, one feeding the other. Although the exact bodily and psychological mechanisms are still not entirely clear, the evidence is mounting that there is some link between psychosocial personality factors and certain forms of cancer, even though the methodological weaknesses in the existing research leave something to be desired.

Most of the research in this field can be subdivided into two categories: those studies which focus on the relationship between various psychometric predispositions and cancer, and those which examine the emotional history or adverse life events and the pathogenesis of cancer.

Personality predispositions and cancer

LeShan (1959) was one of the first to suggest that cancer may result from the loss of a loved one or some significant other, particularly in persons who are prone to feelings of hopelessness, depression, low self-esteem, and introjection. Many of the early researchers in this field have observed that malignancies seem to be associated with what Kissen (1963) and others (Dattore, Shontz, and Coyne, 1980) have termed 'general emotional inhibition, denial and repression'.

LeShan and Worthington (1955) did some of the early work in this field, by comparing 152 cancer patients and 125 patients with other or no illnesses, using a projective test developed by Worthington. The cancer group differed from the control in the following ways: (1) they had difficulty expressing hostile feelings, (2) they suffered the loss of a dear one prior to diagnosis, and (3) they showed greater potential anxiety about the death of a parent.

Kissen (1963) carried out a study among 335 patients, of whom 161 had been diagnosed as having lung cancer, while the others had some other less severe illness. He instrumented a childhood behaviour disorder questionnaire and the Maudsley Personality Inventory, and found that the cancer patients suffered from a 'diminished outlet for emotional discharge', both in their childhood experiences and in their present adult lives. Booth's (1964) Rorschach work on 93 lung cancer patients and 82 tubercular patients revealed similar patterns among the cancer patients. He found that cancer patients responded very differently to the inkblots than tubercular patients, emphasizing emotional repression, the inward direction of anger and the vulnerability to emotional loss.

Studies in the late 1960s and early 1970s used more sophisticated psychometric measures, but still suffered from inadequate or non-representative sampling and inappropriate comparison groups. They nevertheless came up with similar findings to the early work. Pauli and Schmid (1972) carried out an investigation among 57 patients with histologically verified breast cancer and compared them to a group of 34 women with benign disorders of the reproductive organs, using the MMPI. They found that the patients with mastocarcinoma were significantly different on depression, hypochondriasis, and paranoia. Grissom, Weiner, and Weiner (1975) compared healthy subjects and patients with bronchial carcinoma and found that their cancer patients had significantly lower 'personal integration' scores on the Tennessee Self Concept scales. Individuals with this pattern of behaviour frequently direct their frustration, anger, and failure inward, and are vulnerable to the loss of an important relationship.

There have been a great number of studies which have explored the psychometric differences between cancer patients and other patients or normals, but they all suffer from being retrospective. The major problem with these investigations stems from the nature of the primary sample, who are usually diagnosed cancer patients. It is extremely difficult in these circumstances to disentangle the interrelationship between cancer and personality. There is enough evidence available to suggest that the awareness of having cancer can alter various personality measures (Craig and Abeloff, 1974), which could make methodological nonsense of existing findings. Prospective work in this field is now under way in the USA. Paffenbarger (1977), for example, is engaged in a long-term cohort study of over 35,000 former Harvard students and 16,500 University of Pennsylvania students (of both sexes), on whom physiological and psychological data have been accumulating over a large number of years. Much of this work should be ready for publication shortly.

In the meantime, there are a number of premorbid personality studies already available to test some of Kissen's (1963) theories that repression is the fundamental personality mechanism in cancer pathogenesis, particularly in people who have suffered the loss of a love object. To this end, Dattore, Shontz, and Coyne (1980) carried out a very well-designed study of 200 patients (75 cancer and 125 non-cancer patients) on whom premorbid MMPI personality data was available through Veterans Administration Hospital records. Extensive screening of records was involved to ensure comparable samples. They found that the two groups were significantly different on three scales; repression, depression, and denial of hysteria. Their findings on repression were in the direction of earlier studies, that cancer patients showed significantly higher scores. Their results on depression were unexpected but understandable. They found cancer patients had significantly lower depression scores than controls. They argued 'since depression represents such a threatening emotion to the cancer patient, one would expect to see relatively little acknowledgement of depression by subjects in the cancer group'. Similar results were found by Thomas and Greenstreet (1973) in their study of 1076 graduates of Johns Hopkins Medical School. These former students were followed for a number of years, and of the small group who developed cancer, they differed from those who developed other illnesses (e.g. mental illness, hypertension, etc.) and from disease-free controls in being significantly lower on depression and anxiety scales. And finally, Dattore, Shontz, and Coyne (1980) found cancer patients scored lower on the denial-of-hysteria measure, which they interpreted to indicate that they were more *insightful* and *introspective* than non-cancer patients, which is also consistent with earlier theoretical speculations.

While all the results point in a similar direction, the methodological weaknesses here are very great indeed. Most of these studies suffer from inappropriate samples, uncoordinated and unreliable measuring instruments, inadequate comparison groups, retrospective as opposed to prospective data gathering, and a disregard for fitting the research work into any kind of conceptual or theoretical framework. The issue of an appropriate control group is particularly important and the difficulties of interpretation in this respect were highlighted in a recent study by Watson and Schuld (1977). They took a sample of cancer patients and matched control groups, and found no significant differences on any of the MMPI scales between the two. Although the data was collected on a premorbid basis (i.e. well before any clinical diagnosis of cancer), the sample was comprised of individuals for whom psychopathology had been diagnosed (i.e. they were psychiatric patients). In addition, the malignancy group contained a large proportion of people with alcohol-related problems, six times as many as in the control group (Kellerman, 1978). These kinds of studies create a great deal of confusion in the cancer field and could be controlled by more careful research designs. As Perrin and Pierce (1959) suggest, each study of cancer and personality should contain ideally two control groups, one of subjects who have some chronic, non-cancerous disease sufficient to cause him/her anxiety about his/her health, and the other a comparison group of 'healthy' subjects.

Life events and cancer

A second category of studies in this field has focused on recent stressful life events and the onset of cancer. In this respect, the Holmes and Rahe (1967) Social Readjustment Rating Scale (SRRS) has been used extensively as a measuring tool. There are several problems with this instrument, which may make the research in this area less fruitful than it could otherwise be. First, the SRRS lists a number of events which may be symptoms or consequences of illness rather than critical incidences (e.g. change in number of marital arguments, fired from work, sex difficulties, etc.). Second, each event on the SRRS has differential meaning for each subject, yet they are rigidly enumerated in scoring. And finally, the illness itself may impede or prevent the patient from accurately recalling past events, as Napier, Metzner, and Johnson (1972) have found.

Nevertheless, a great deal of attention has been directed to life events research. Indeed, in LeShan's (1959) early review of 75 studies on psychological factors in the development of malignant disease, he concluded 'the most consistently reported, relevant psychological factor has been the loss of a major emotional relationship prior to the first-noted symptoms of neoplasm'. He later carried out a large-scale epidemiological study (LeShan, 1966) into mortality rates among different groups of people likely to be affected by loss of a close emotional relationship. He predicted that cancer mortality rates should be highest for widowed, next highest for divorced, and lowest for married and then single persons, if the theory of loss of emotional relationships are valid. He analysed epidemiological data from a number of studies, age-adjusting the mortality rates, and found that the data was consistent with this hypothesis.

Muslin, Gyarfas, and Pieper (1966) carried out an investigation of 165 women who were about to have a breast biopsy. They were interviewed and given a life-events questionnaire prior to diagnosis, and in the end they were able to produce 37 matched pairs of malignant and benign subjects. They found that twice as many diagnosed cancer patients had 'a permanent loss of a first degree relative or other person whom the subject specifically stated was emotionally important to her', than did the benign group.

Schmale and Iker (1966) explored the same phenomena among a group of women who were reporting for a cone biopsy as a result of a positive Pap test. They were given psychological tests and interviewed prior to diagnosis and none of the subjects had any gross abnormality that would lead the physician to suspect cervical cancer. On the basis of high life-events scores six months prior to the first positive Pap smear, the authors then predicted who would ultimately be diagnosed as having cervical cancer. It was found that there was a significantly high level of accuracy in their judgements, based almost solely on life events immediately preceding the first tests.

In recent years, a great deal of sustained work has been carried out by Greer and his colleagues (Greer and Morris, 1975; Greer, 1979). In a recent study on premorbid breast cancer, Greer (1979) studied 160 women admitted to hospital for a breast tumor biopsy . . . a breast tumor was defined as being 'a tumour with or without palpable axillary nodes, with no deep attachment and no distant metastases', that is, women with either very early breast cancer which is operable, or with some breast disease which is benign. These patients were interviewed on the day prior to the biopsy and detailed information was collected on stressful life events (e.g. events which caused them severe and prolonged emotional distress). These events were verified by husbands or close relatives. Additional psychometric data was also collected on depression, hostility, extraversion/neuroticism, and other social and psychiatric states. After the operation, 69 were found to have breast cancer and 91 a benign breast disease. The cancer and controls (i.e. benign group) were matched in most respects (e.g. social class, marital state, etc.) except that the cancer patients were significantly older.

No significant differences were found in respect of the occurrence of stressful life events, including loss of a loved person, depression, or denial as the characteristic response to life stresses. Although an effort was made to design the research in a way that would minimize the effects of diagnosed cancer on personality and the recall of life events, the author admits himself that 'we had no control over what surgeons told patients before admission'. In addition, he was unable to control for the fear of having an operation which could result in the removal of a breast and the diagnosis of breast cancer. As well, the cancer group were significantly older, which could have biased the results. But most important of all, since breast cancer may take several years to develop and the stressful life events responsible may take place years before that, there is a strong potential 'memory falsification' problem. What is really needed, as Greer himself suggests, are large-scale prospective studies with more sophisticated control groups.

There have been other studies which have explored traumatic life events and cancer, without using the SRRS. For example, Smith and Sebastian (1976) examined the emotional history of 44 cancer patients and 44 patients with physical abnormalities which were non-cancerous. Structured interviews were carried out to try and identify the frequency, intensity, and duration of emotional states in each person's life, which involved questions about family life, childhood, social and sexual life, career, religion, etc. Their approach was far more open-ended than the traditional life-events research just reviewed, in that they relied on interview responses to the following question:

> I am going to ask you to remember events that have occurred in your life which have made you feel very concerned, emotional, stressed and so forth. I will ask you to relate the kind of events that provoked emotional feelings in you, the date of the event and the intensity and duration of the events and emotional conditions. We will begin with early childhood and end up with questions about your present life situation.

Critical incidents were then recorded and rated as either high, medium, or low, and the intensity and duration of the emotional events for each person were rated on a 15 point scale. It was found that there was significantly more frequent and intense emotional events prior to diagnosis among cancer patients than in the comparison group.

Another interesting study along these lines was undertaken by Witzel (1970) among 150 cancer patients and 150 patients with other serious diseases. He took personal histories of past illnesses and found that non-cancer patients had a significantly larger number of reported incidents of medical problems throughout their lives than cancer patients. They reported being out-patients three times more often than cancer patients, being in a hospital bed three times more often, having temperatures in excess of 38.5°C seven times more often, and experiencing twice as many minor illnesses and operations. The authors contend that this does not necessarily contradict the other research on adverse life events, because these critical medical incidents may signal the disease process itself. As Fox (1978) has suggested, 'developing cancer had mobilised the immune response, which is capable of fighting many diseases, and which, because of its aroused status, could do so more successfully than that of non-cancer patients'.

The area of stressful life events and the pathogenesis of cancer is a potentially fruitful field of future research and must be seriously considered. At the very least, adverse life events must act as an intervening, if not primary source, of illness behaviour. As Haney (1977) has recently suggested,

> adverse life events may produce situations and circumstances which heighten the individual's belief in his susceptibility or increase the perceived threat. Adverse life events may exacerbate existing, and often otherwise well tolerated symptoms and reduce the individual's tendency to deny them or delay help-seeking.

Currie (1974) aptly sums up the present state of research by saying, in the context of tumour immunology but which applies equally well to the field of cancer and the psychological processes: 'our knowledge . . . is primitive because the methodology is primitive. With the development of refined . . . methods, will come a refinement in our knowledge of the subject.'

Stress and Working Women

The role of women in society is radically changing in most Western countries (Hall and Hall, 1980). Vast numbers of women are beginning to work full-time and to aspire to climb the same 'organizational ladders' as their male counterparts (Hennig and Jardim, 1978). Indeed, the latest figures from the US Department of Labour indicate that the 'typical American family' with a working husband, a homemaker wife, and two children, now makes up only 7% of all US families. In addition, whereas in 1960, 31% of all married women in the US were working, as were 19% of women with children under six, by 1975 the comparable figures were substantially higher at 44% and 37% respectively.

A similar trend is occuring in the UK, with the male labour force increasing at the rate of only 3% over the last 25 years, whereas in the same period the number of women employed has grown at 43%. In addition, in the early 1950s there were 2.7 million married women in jobs, but by 1976 that figure had risen by 143% to over 6.7 million. And most interesting of all, at the start of the 1950s only a quarter of working women were married, whereas today over two-thirds of all women who are working are married.

But what does this trend mean for the health and well-being of women? Will they join the growing number of men who suffer from stress-related illnesses as a result of work? In England and Wales, for example, the death rate due to coronary heart disease in men between 35 and 44 nearly doubled between 1950 and 1973, and has increased much more rapidly than that of older age ranges (e.g. 45 to 54). Indeed, by 1973, 41% of all deaths in the age group 25 to 44 were due to cardiovascular disease (Cooper, 1981). Will women who take on full-time careers and those who take on traditionally male jobs, therefore, end up with the 'male diseases of work'.

Growing body of research

More and more research work is being conducted to answer this question and although there are medics who feel that working women are less at risk than men (*Lancet*, 1980), the early studies in this field are disturbing. One of the most interesting and comprehensive investigations was recently carried out by Haynes and Feinleib (1980). Their sample was drawn from the Framingham Heart Study, which is the most comprehensive investigation of heart disease ever carried out. Inhabitants of Framingham, Massachusetts, have been undergoing regular medical screening for the past twenty years. The main purpose of the study is to identify the precursors to heart disease in this population. Interested to see what the impact of employment is on working women, Haynes and Feinleib collected data on the employment status and behaviour of 350 housewives, 387 working women (employed outside the home for over one-half of their adult years), and 580 men (between the ages of 45 and 64) in the Framingham Study. All 1317 subjects in the investigation were followed for the development of coronary heart disease over an eight-year period.

Their main finding was that working women did not have a significantly higher incidence of coronary heart disease than housewives, and their rates were lower than for working men. They then analysed the data in terms of married (including divorced, widowed, and separated) versus single working women, and found a substantial increase in incidence of heart disease. But the most revealing of all their results appeared when they compared married working women with children, against those without children. In this case they found that 'among working women, the incidence of coronary heart disease rose as the number of children increased'. This was not the case, however, for women who were housewives; indeed, that group showed a slight decrease with an increasing number of children.

In addition to these results, they also found that working women as a whole 'experienced more daily stress, marital dissatisfaction, and aging worries and were less likely to show overt anger than either housewives or men'. Indeed, in a review of the research literature on marital adjustment in dual-career marriages, Staines, *et al.* (1978) found that of the 13 major studies in this area, using either a US national or regional sample, at least 11 of them showed that marital adjustment was worse for dual-career wives than for non-working wives.

On the other hand, Newberry, Weissman, and Myers (1980) examined the psychiatric status and social adjustment of a matched group of working married women and housewives drawn from a community sample. They used the Social Adjustment Scale, Gurin's Symptom Check List, and the Schedule for Affective Disorders and Schizophrenia. They found that although there was no difference between the two groups on overall psychiatric symptoms, depressive symptoms, diagnosable psychiatric disorders or treatment for an emotional problem in the past year, married working women did differ from housewives in their attitudes toward work and the home. Indeed, they found that housewives suffered from greater 'work impairment', feelings of inadequacy, disinterest, and overall work maladjustment than working wives. On the other hand, working wives were found to be more impaired, disinterested, and inadequate in respect of their housework as compared to their work.

Although there is some scattered evidence, as above, that working women may not be 'at risk' of stress-related illness or other negative social consequences, the data is beginning to mount to the contrary, particularly for working women who are married with a family. In a study of psychiatric disorders among professional women, Welner et al. (1979) found, for example, that women GPs had a significantly higher rate of psychiatric depression than a control, and that women with children were found to have significantly more career disruption than those without children. In addition, Cooper and Davidson (1982) found that married female executives with children were under greater stress than single or divorced working women. Indeed, Hall and Hall (1980) suggest that the main source of stress among two-career couples stems from the fact that the number of demands on the partners exceeds the time and energy to deal with them. Families, in this context, add a further series of potential problem areas, particularly when organizations are doing very little, if anything, to help the dual-career family, and specifically the wife who is expected to play 'mother' and 'worker'.

Aside from these findings, some startling results are beginning to emerge from the total Framingham sample in regard to Type A coronary-prone behaviour and women. Two distinguished cardiologists, Friedman and Rosenman (1974) showed a significant relationship between behavioural patterns of people and their prevalence to stress-related illness, particularly coronary heart disease. Type A behaviour is characterized by 'extremes of competitiveness, striving for achievement, aggressiveness, haste, impatience, restlessness, hyperalertness, explosiveness of speech, tenseness of facial muscles, feelings of being under pressure of time and under the challenge of responsibility'. Type B behaviour, on the other hand, is characterized by the relative absence of the behaviour associated with Type A individuals. On the basis of large-scale prospective research work, Rosenman, Friedman and Strauss (1966) found that this Type A behaviour pattern in all groups of people is a significant precursor to coronary heart disease and other stress-related illnesses: Type A men in the age groups 39–49 and 50–59 had 6.5

and 1.9 times (respectively) the incidence of coronary heart disease than Type B men.

In this context, one interesting finding that is beginning to emerge from the Framingham Study is that working women who score high on Type A are *twice* as likely to develop coronary heart disease than their male Type A counterparts. Indeed, a recent study in the UK (Davidson and Cooper, 1980) found that senior female executives had significantly higher Type A behaviour scores than male executives, which in terms of these Framingham results may mean that female professional women may be at greater risk of actual coronaries than many of the 'captains of industry'.

The next question that must be asked is 'why do working women suffer more than non-working women and in some respects more than their male colleagues?' This is a vital research question of the future. But, it has been hypothesized that one explanation is that most working women are expected, without much support from their husbands, to fulfil the roles of both home-maker and career person simultaneously (Hall and Hall, 1980). Although many husbands of working women *intellectually* accept and encourage their wives in their careers, few either psychologically or practically (e.g. by taking on traditional housewife's chores) support them. When one considers that most males come from homes where their role model was a 'mother at home', the fact that they still expect their working wives to carry out the traditional household duties is not surprising.

In addition, most work organizations have not adequately planned for the increasing desire of women both to work and to have a family; it is this social myopia which is creating enormous pressure on working women.

Putting aside all moral arguments, it is in the long-term economic interest of work organizations to begin to accommodate to the needs of the increasing army of women at work, particularly the married ones with families. If future stress research can identify these dual roles as a problem area for women, then there are a number of strategies available to private and public-sector organizations to help alleviate some of the unnecessary burdens of working women. It might be helpful to outline some of these here.

What Organizations Can Do

In his recent book, Cooper (1981) highlights the kind of strategies that might help to minimize the problems of working women and dual-career couples in general, which should prepare a firmer foundation to alleviate home–work interface stresses and strains.

Flexible working arrangements

There are a wide range of flexible working arrangements that organizations can provide their male and female employees which can help them to accommodate to changing family patterns. *Flexitime* is obviously one good example. In order that a dual-career wife or husband can meet the psychological responsibilities associated with their children's education, or indeed, free themselves of guilt, many parents feel that they must take their children to school and/or pick them up. This is very difficult to accomplish under the current 9 to 5 (or later) arrangement, and would be made much easier under flexitime conditions — as long as it was applicable for both husband and wife. Flexitime is not only useful during the work week, but why shouldn't it be extended to 'school vacation' times? Many dual-career parents are concerned about arrangements for their children during the summer months when they are at home. There are several ways of coping with this problem: allowing the dual wife or husband to have a lighter load during these months, allowing them to build up a backlog of working time during other months to relieve them during these; providing facilities on site during the summer months for young children (perhaps by the use of university students training in the field of primary education), or some combination of these.

Another more flexible working arrangement would be more *part-time work* in a variety of different forms: limiting the number of days a week, or hours in a day, or indeed in shortening the work week by allowing individuals to work three- or four-day, forty-hour weeks. This last suggestion is growing in popularity and if dual husband and wife were able to do this they could, by careful planning, easily manage their domestic and work arrangements between them. In 1972 an American Management Association survey estimated that between 700 and 1000 firms of over 100 000 employees *in toto* were on a four-day, forty-hour week in the USA. By 1975, the number of firms grew to 3000, covering over one million workers. Indeed, many firms are moving to a three-day, thirty-eight-hour week without decline in productivity and job satisfaction (Foster *et al.*, 1979).

Allied to many of these suggestions is the notion that organizations provide creche or nursery facilities in the workplace. There is increasing growth of these in many of the 'advanced thinking' organizations. Many educationalists and psychologists have felt this is a good idea, since it provides the mother or father with the opportunity of seeing their children some time during working hours. A less satisfactory solution would be community-based nurseries, but these may be necessary for those who work for small companies or who are self-employed. The benefits that organizations could derive from the introduction of 'industrial kibbutzim' seems so obvious that it is surprising that more companies have not followed suit.

Working at home

With the advent of the microprocessor revolution, it should become increasingly easier for dual husbands and wives in certain types of jobs to work at home. The need for a central workplace should decrease quite dramatically over the next decade or two. Already, employees can take home a computer terminal, or indeed a minicomputer itself, to carry out many of the tasks that they were once only able to do in a centralized work environment. In order to be able to do this, work organizations will have to rid themselves of their deep-rooted, nefarious suspicion of their employees, that is, that they will take every opportunity to exploit their employer and work as little as possible; and only by overseeing them will work get done! Indeed it is this very control that has made the process of work for many unsatisfying and has encouraged compartmentalization of work and home life to the detriment of the former. As C. Wright Mills has suggested: 'Each day men sell little pieces of themselves in order to try and buy them back each night and weekend with little pieces of fun.'

Some organizations may one day realize that they may not need a centralized workplace at all. For the time being, however, work organizations ought to explore the variety of jobs that could easily be done at home and provide this degree of flexibility to their employees. At the very least, it is worth an experiment!

Smoothing the way for women

Many women who have played the traditional family 'caring' role, need particular help if they are to change the pattern of their marriage and fulfil a more dual role. One problem these women may face, after many years away from work, is lack of confidence and feeling that they are out of date (or, in fact, actually are out of date). It is in the interest of employers and the wider community to provide opportunities for such women to be brought up-to-date with current developments. This might best be done by professional associations, or indeed by work organizations providing updating courses for ex-employees who have temporarily left employment to raise a family. As Fogarty, Rapoport, and Rapoport (1971) have suggested: 'The important thing in the interests of both employers and of young mothers themselves is to minimize the interruption to a highly qualified women's career and to keep her as closely in touch as possible with her particular world of work.' Any help the industrial organization can give its former employees in maintaining their skills may pay off greatly in the future, not only in terms of 'good will' but also in reducing costs of retraining or initial training of needed new staff. As far as the question of confidence is concerned, this can be done during the updating activity or by specialized courses prior to retraining or updating, depending on the time gap between the termination of full employment and 'the return'.

Maternity and paternity leave

It is obvious that what many women at work need, if they are preparing to have a family, is some sense of security about their job. In this respect it only seems sensible to have some reasonable maternity leave with a guaranteed right to return to work after it, and with some financial security during the leave period. Most countries in the European Common Market have guarantees against dismissal during pregnancy, a guarantee of paid maternity leave (usually between eight and twelve weeks and up to six months in many Eastern European countries) and guarantees of the right to return to work either immediately following the paid maternity leave period or unpaid leave after some prearranged return period (in some cases up to two or three years later). Different countries have different arrangements in this respect.

Paternity leave is also particularly important in the changing circumstances of the family. Few organizations provide this contemporary innovation, but many will have to consider it in the near future if they want to deal more systematically with what may end up, if ignored, as an uncontrolled absenteeism problem in the future. Dual-career families will increasingly need the flexibility of short-leave periods, and the provision of leave for both men and women should help to ease the problem.

If we can begin to redesign our work organizations to meet the challenges of the social changes in our society, we may be able to avoid Studs Terkel's (1972) lament in the Introduction, 'work is, by its very nature, about violence . . . to the spirit as well as to the body. It is about ulcers as well as accidents, about shouting matches as well as fistfights, about nervous breakdowns as well as kicking the dog around. It is, above all (or beneath all), about daily humiliations.'

References

Booth, G. (1964) *Cancer and Culture: Psychological Disposition and Environment.* (A Rorschach Study). Unpublished.
Cooper, C. L. (1981) *The Stress Check.* New Jersey: Prentice-Hall Inc.
Cooper, C. L., and Marshall, J. (1976) Occupational sources of stress. *Journal of Occupational Psychology*, **49**, 11–28.
Cooper, C. L., and Davidson, M. (1982) *High Pressure: The Working Lives of Women Managers.* London: Fontana.
Craig, T. J., and Abeloff, M. D. (1974) Psychiatric symptomatology among hospitalised cancer patients. *American Journal of Psychiatry*, **131**, 1323–7.
Currie, G. A. (1974) *Cancer and the Immune Response.* London: Edward Arnold.
Dattore, P., Shontz, F., and Coyne, L. (1980) Premorbid personality differentiation of cancer and non-cancer groups. *Journal of Consulting and Clinical Psychology*, **48**(3), 388–94.

Davidson, M., and Cooper, C. L. (1980) Type A coronary prone behaviour and stress in senior female managers and administrators. *Journal of Occupational Medicine*, **22**, 801–6.

Evans, E. (1926) *A Psychological Study of Cancer*. New York: Dodd-Mead.

Fogarty, M. P., Rapoport, R., and Rapoport, R. N. (1971) *Sex, Career and Family*. Beverly Hills: Sage.

Foster, L. W., Latack, J. C., and Riendl, L. J. (1979) The effects and promises of the shortened work week. *Proceedings of the Academy of Management Annual Conference*, August 1979.

Fox, B. H. (1978) Premorbid psychological factors as related to cancer incidence. *Journal of Behavioural Medicine*, **1**(1), 45–133.

Friedman, M., and Rosenman, R. H. (1974) *Type A Behaviour and Your Heart*. London: Wildwood House.

Glass, D. (1977) *Behaviour Patterns, Stress and Coronary Disease*. New Jersey: LEA.

Greenberg, H. (1980) *Coping with Job Stress*. New Jersey: Prentice-Hall Inc.

Greer, S. (1979) Psychological enquiry: a contribution to cancer research. *Journal of Psychological Medicine*, **9**, 81–9.

Greer, S., and Morris, T. (1975) Psychological attributes of women who develop breast cancer: a controlled study. *Journal of Psychosomatic Research*, **19**, 147–53.

Grissom, J., Weiner, B., and Weiner, E. (1975) Psychological correlates of cancer. *Journal of Consulting and Clinical Psychology*, **43**, 113.

Hall, D. T., and Hall, F. (1980) Stress and the two career couple. In Cooper, C. L., and Payne, R. (Eds), *Current Concerns in Occupational Stress*, London: John Wiley Sons.

Haney, C. A. (1977) Illness behaviour and psychosocial correlates of cancer. *Journal of Social Science and Medicine*, **11**(4), 223–8.

Haynes, S. G., and Feinleib, M. (1980) Women, work and coronary heart disease: prospective findings from the Framingham Heart Study. *American Journal of Public Health*, **70**, 133–41.

Haynes, S., Feinleib, M., and Kannel, W. (1980) The relationship of psychological factors to coronary heart disease in the Framingham Study. *American Journal of Epidemiology*, **111**(1), 37–58.

Hennig, M., and Jardim, A. (1978) *The Managerial Woman*. London: Pan Books.

Holmes, T. H., and Rahe, R. H. (1967) The social readjustment rating scale. *The Journal of Psychosomatic Medicine*. **11**, 213–18.

Kellerman, J. (1978) A note on psychosomatic factors. *Journal of Consulting and Clinical Psychology*, **46**, 1522–3.

Kissen, D. (1963) Personality characteristics in males conducive to lung cancer. *British Journal of Medical Psychology*, **36**, 27–36.

Kissen, D. (1969) The present state of psychosomatic cancer research. *Geriatrics*, **24**, 129.

Lancet (1980) Editorial: Women, work and coronary heart disease, July 12, 76–7.

LeShan, L. (1959) Psychological states as factors in the development of malignant disease: A critical review. *Journal of the National Cancer Institute*, **22**, 1–18.

LeShan, L. (1966) An emotional life-history pattern associated with neoplastic disease. *Annual New York Academy of Science Journal*, **125**, 780–93.

LeShan, L., and Worthington, R. E., (1955) Some psychological correlates of neoplastic disease: preliminary report. *Journal of Clinical and Experimental Psychopathology*, **16**, 281.

Muslin, H. L., Gyarfas, K., and Pieper, W. J. (1966) Separation experience and cancer of the breast. *Annual New York Academy of Science Journal*, **125**, 802–6.

Napier, J. A., Metzner, H., and Johnson, B. C. (1972) Limitations of morbidity and mortality data obtained from family histories: A report from the Tecumseh studies. *American Journal of Public Health*, **62**, 30–5.

Newberry, P., Weissman, M., and Myers, J. (1980) Working wives and housewives: do they differ in mental status and social adjustment? *American Journal of Orthopsychiatry*, **49**, 282–91.

Paffenbarger, R. S. (1977) Psychosocial factors in students predictive of cancer, *Grant No. 1RO1 CA 225 74–01 National Cancer Institute*, Bethesda, Md.

Pauli, H., and Schmid, V. (1972) Psychosomatic aspects in the clinical manifestation of mastocarcinoma. *Journal of Psychotherapy and Medical Psychology*, **22**(2).

Perrin, G. M.., and Pierce, I. R. (1959) Psychosomatic aspects of cancer: A review. *Psychosomatic Medicine*, **5**, 397–421.

Rosenman, R., Friedman, M., and Jenkins, C. D. (1967) Clinically unrecognised myocardial infarction in the Western Collaborative Group Study. *American Journal of Cardiology*, **19**, 776–82.

Rosenman, R. H., Friedman, M., and Strauss, R. (1966) CHD in the Western Collaborative Group Study. *Journal of the American Medical Association*, **195**, 86–92.

Schmale, A. H., and Iker, H. P. (1966) The affect of hopelessness and the development of cancer. *Journal of Psychosomatic Medicine*, **28**, 714–21.

Selye, H. (1979) Correlating stress and cancer. *American Journal of Proctology, Gastroenterology, Colon and Rectal Surgery*, **30**(4), 18–28.

Smith, W. R., and Sebastian, H. (1976) Emotional history and pathogenesis of cancer. *Journal of Clinical Psychology*, **32**(4), 63–6.

Snow, H. (1893) *Cancer and the Cancer Process*. London: Churchill.

Staines, G. L., Pleck, J. H., Shepard, L., and O'Connor, P. (1978) Wives' employment status and marital adjustment. *Working Paper*, Institute of Social Research, University of Michigan.

Terkel, S. (1972) *Working*. New York: Avon Books.

Thomas, C. B., and Greenstreet, R. L. (1973) Psychobiological characteristics in youth as predictors of five disease states: Suicide, mental illness, hypertension, coronary heart disease and tumor. *John Hopkins Medical Journal*, **132**, 16–43.

Watson, C., and Schuld, D. (1977) Psychosomatic factors in the etiology of neoplasmas. *Journal of Consulting and Clinical Psychology*, **45**(3), 455–61.

Welner, A., Marten, S., Wochnick, E., Davis, M., Fishman, R., and Clayton, J. (1979) Psychiatric disorders among professional women. *Archives of General Psychiatry*, **36**, 169–73.

Witzel, L. (1970) Anamnese und Zweiterkrankungen bei Patienten mit bosartigen Neubildungen ('Anamnesis and second diseases in patients with malignant tumors'). *Med. Klin.* **65**, 876–9.

Note:

Parts of this chapter have been published in the *Bulletin of the British Psychological Society*, the author would like to thank the B.P.S.

Stress Research
Edited by Cary L. Cooper
© 1983, John Wiley & Sons, Ltd.

Chapter 6
Stress, Disease, and Personality: The 'Inoculation Effect'[1]

H. J. Eysenck
Professor of Psychology, Institute of Psychiatry, University of London, UK

The Stress–Personality Paradigm

The hypothesis that some diseases are caused by stress, and may be related to certain aspects of personality, has been widely accepted, although the evidence for it is not always very convincing. Many physicians over the centuries, relying on personal experience and insight, have postulated such relationships (Eysenck, 1980), but the notion of 'psychosomatic disorders' only became widely accepted through the advocacy of dynamically oriented investigators. The tangled history of this concept in the last thirty years or so tells of methodological inadequacy, theoretical incompatibility, and experimental poverty. Freudian theories, even in the original domain of neurotic disorders, are essentially difficult to falsify, and even when they have proved contrary to the factual evidence have seldom been admitted to be wrong by psychoanalysts (Eysenck and Wilson, 1973). It will not be one of the purposes of this chapter to engage in a critique of psychoanalytic ideas, but rather to try and indicate the direction in which more scientific research might go, the kinds of theories susceptible to proof or disproof, and some of the findings which may suggest the desirability of further research (Eysenck, 1981a).

The concepts of 'stress' and 'personality' are usually considered as quite separate, but this is a grievous error. They are closely related, for two main reasons. In the first place, the very notion of 'stress' cannot be understood without the specification of the particular organism involved in the supposedly stressful situation. The experimental literature is full of demonstrations that situations which are experienced as 'stressful' by one person (say an introvert) are experienced as pleasant by another (say an extravert). Thus parties and many other social situations would fall into this group. *Stress* can only be defined in terms of *strain* experienced by the individual, and identical

situations may or may not give rise to strain in different individuals. There
are definite theories relating personality to stress, many of which have received strong experimental support (Eysenck, 1967, 1981a); we will refer
back to some of these later on.

The other reason why stress and personality are so closely related can best
be understood by a simple comparison with physics. Let us consider Hooke's
law of elasticity: stress = $k \times$ strain, where k is a constant (the modulus of
elasticity) that depends on the nature of material and type of stress used to
produce the strain. This constant k, i.e. the stress/strain ratio, is called
Young's modulus, and is illustrated (with certain simplifications) in Figure 1.
A and B are two metals differing in elasticity; they are stressed by increasing
loads, and the elongation corresponding to each load is plotted on the
abscissa. It will be seen that identical loads give rise to quite divergent
elongations, α and β. Thus the physicist does not have the simple stimulus
(independent variable)–response (dependent variable) relationship; it also

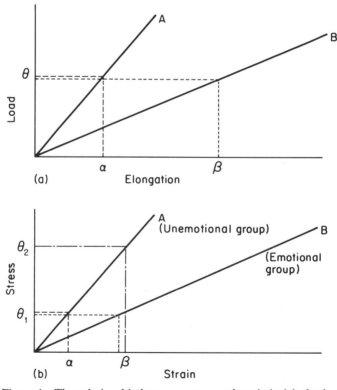

Figure 1   The relationship between stress and strain in (a) physics
and (b) psychology

incorporates the term k, which corresponds to the notion of *organism* in psychology. The more recent formulation: S-O-R (stress-organism-response) attempts to do justice to this situation, but such a formulation certainly carries with it the implication that we ought to change our functional law to read: $a = f(b, O)$. In other words, a is a function not only of b, but also of the particular nature of the *organism* which is being stimulated, just as the elongation of the wire in the experiment detailed in Figure (a) is a function partly of the nature of the wire, partly of the weight used to stretch it. As far as physics is concerned, strain would correspond to the experimental method, k to the 'individual differences' or correlational method, and no physicist would ever doubt that both are essential for a united science (Eysenck, 1975).

Let us use the same argument in relation to psychology. Figure 1(b) illustrates an analysis of human behaviour (physiological, verbal, expressive) in an experimental situation productive of emotion. Again the stress (independent variable) is plotted on the ordinate, and the strain (dependent variable) on the abscissa; A and B represent an emotionally stable and an emotionally unstable individual, or group of individuals respectively. Identical stress θ_1 gives rise to quite different strains α and β. It would require stress θ_2 to make the strain in A individuals equal to that produced by θ_1 in B individuals. Differences between θ_1 and θ_2 are the kinds of differences traditionally studied by experimental psychologists; differences between A and B are the kinds of differences traditionally studied by personality psychologists, believers in the importance of constitutional factors, and clinical psychologists. In order to understand what is going on, in order to formulate theories, and to make predictions, we must incorporate both types of factors in our model.

This model may be called compensatory or substitutional, in the sense that one type of variable can compensate for or be substituted for the other (Savage and Eysenck, 1964). To produce a certain elongation greater than x we can either increase the weight suspended from the wire, or we can choose a wire whose k indicates greater pliability. On the human side, consider a series of experiments carried out by Rosenbaum (1953, 1956). He found that threat of a strong shock led to greater generalization of a voluntary response than did threat of a weak shock; this would be a typical experimental approach. He also discovered that anxious subjects showed greater generalization to *identical* stimuli than did non-anxious subjects; this would be the typical correlational or individual-differences approach. (It is interesting to note that Rosenbaum published one paper in the *Journal of Experimental Psychology*, the other in the *Journal of Abnormal and Social Psychology*, thus ensuring that very few psychologists would read *both* papers!) To obtain a given degree of generalization, we can thus either change the strength of the threatened shock, or choose more or less anxious subjects; the two can be traded against each other. Savage and Eysenck (1964) have carried out a series of experiments with rats, illustrating the same point. Their chapter is headed 'Definition and measurement of emotionality', indicating another important function of this whole theoretical concept of experimental and individual-differences variables as being to some degree interchangeable.

We may ask ourselves whether a given test or measure which is used to indicate differences in emotionality or anxiety, whether in humans or in animals, is in fact a good measure of that variable, and this whole question of validity of tests has of course always been a very difficult one. It can be solved, however, along the lines of the above argument, by looking at experiments which are generally accepted as increasing an organism's degree of emotionality. We can then argue that if experimental modification x could produce an increment in emotionality, which can be indexed by performance y, then if our personality test is a good measure of emotion or anxiety, people having high scores on this test should behave like persons subjected to a strong dose of x, i.e. show strong y, whereas people having low scores on a should have low scores on y. Thus, this conception of the relationship between experimental and individual differences variables gives us a powerful tool for demonstrating the validity of personality measures, adding substantially to the range of application of the experimental design.

Another important consequence of these theoretical considerations is that if the suggestions made above are true, then it follows that we cannot make verifiable predictions from general laws without incorporating specifically a variable k which refers to the constitution of the individual for whom the prediction is being made. Consider an experiment reported by Jensen (1962). He studied the number of errors in serial learning as a function of the rate of stimulus presentation; there were two rates, one of 2 seconds, and one of 4 seconds. The traditional experimental psychologist would regard this problem as meaningful and soluble; either differences in rate of stimulus presentation cause a difference in the number of errors to criterion, or they do not. Jensen argued that this test imposes a stress on the subject, and that the resulting stress would be indexed in terms of an increased number of errors when the shorter rate of stimulus presentation was employed, as compared with the longer rate. (There is an obvious pressure with the quick rate of presentation which might well increase the general stress of the test situation.)

This stress would impose differential strain on the individuals respectively high and low on trait anxiety, and Jensen measured this trait anxiety with the neuroticism scale of the Maudsley Personality Inventory (MPI). Contrasting subjects scoring high and low respectively on this scale, he found that for low scorers (i.e. nonemotional individuals) the added stress of shortening the rate of stimulus presentation produced no effect at all; they made

63 errors on the average for the long rate, and 64 errors for the short rate. But for the high scorers there was a tremendous difference; during the long rate of presentation they only made 46 errors, i.e. far fewer than the unemotional subjects, while for the short rate of presentation they made 90 errors. In other words, the results of the experiment can only be understood in terms of the person–condition interaction; leaving out the differential personality effect makes complete nonsense out of any simple averaging of the results. Such averaging would tell us that there was a mild and nonsignificant effect of shortening the rate of presentation, when in reality there was no effect for nonemotional subjects, and a very strong effect for emotional ones.

I feel very strongly that just as it would be meaningless in physics to leave out the constant k in dealing with predictions of the kind considered, so it is meaningless in psychology to try and frame general laws without taking into account individual differences. In fact, this is even more so in psychology than in physics, because of certain very relevant differences between these two sciences. In physics we can usually proceed along very analytic lines, by experimentally excluding certain variables, and by completely dissecting the objects of our interest, until we are dealing with simple elements or alloys of known composition. In psychology, however, we cannot do this. By definition, we are dealing with organisms and their behaviour; as a consequence we are not allowed to cut up the organism in such a way as to isolate certain aspects. The integrity of the organism must be maintained, and that means inevitably that the personality, the intelligence, and other important functions of the organism will play an important part in whatever measurement we may be concerned with. To relegate these individual differences to the error term, as experimentalists are wont to do, simply means that the error term will become enormously exaggerated in size, and the main effects (unless in trivial and obvious experiments) will be much smaller than is acceptable in a scientific discipline. We can rescue these variables from the error term by looking at interactions, and many experiments have shown that these interaction terms can frequently be much more important than the so-called main effects (Eysenck, 1967, 1981a). This general rule has certain important consequences for the design of experiments meant to test perfectly general hypotheses in experimental psychology, which have been spelled out and illustrated elsewhere (Eysenck, 1976). The many different experiments quoted to illustrate this point, suggest that the use of personality parameters in experimental psychology is not only permissive but *mandatory* (Eysenck, 1981a). An experiment in which personality variables are theoretically likely to play a part should never be planned without either including these personality variables in the analysis of variance design, or at least measuring them in order to use them as moderator variables in the final analysis.

Cancer, Stress, and Personality

We have seen that the relationship between stress and strain requires the introduction of individual-differences variables, and that personality variables like neuroticism can be demonstrated experimentally to fill this role. We have seen that stress and personality can be used interchangeably, in the sense that a high N (neurotic) personality will react with strain to stress stimuli which do not produce strain in low N individuals, so that it might be said that *ceteris paribus* high N individuals live a more stressful life, not in the sense that they necessarily encounter more stressful stimuli (although that may be so) but because identical stressful stimuli produce a greater amount of strain in them. This generalization is almost certainly a gross oversimplification of a very complex situation, but it may help us to produce testable hypotheses in relation to disease. We will discuss first of all cancer, and then cardiovascular disease, in relation to deductions which may be made from this hypothesis.

Taking cancer first, we will first look at the question of *stress*. The implication of stress parameters in cancer has been surveyed at length by Sklar and Anisman (1981), and the field is certainly a very complex one. There is, to begin with, the distinction between chronic and acute stress; there is, secondly, the distinction between avoidable and unavoidable stress; and there is, thirdly, the problem of coping mechanisms. In relation to the disease itself, we cannot just talk about 'cancer', but must deal with the several phases involved, i.e. tumour induction, tumour growth, and metastases. Clearly this chapter is not the place to go into any details, for which the reader is referred to the review just cited; we will simply attempt to present an outline of a view which, while testable, is at the moment a little more than a theory linking together some more or less firmly established facts.

Stress

In relation to the development of cancer in humans, retrospective studies have shown that life stress events frequently precede the appearance of forms of neoplasia, e.g. Bahnson and Bahnson, 1969; Greene, 1966; Horne and Picard, 1979; Jacobs and Charles, 1980. Greene and Swisher (1969) succeeded in eliminating genetic factors by looking at leukaemia in monozygotic twins discordant for the illness, and found that psychological stress was an important feature in the origins of this disease. Reviews by Bloom, Asher, and White (1978) and Fox (1978) give a good survey of the literature.

One of the stressors most frequently studied has been loss of spouse, and here again there are a number of studies (Bloom, Asher, and White, 1978; Greene, 1966; LeShan, 1966; Lombard and Potter, 1950; Murphy, 1952;

Peller, 1952; Ernster *et al.*, 1979) showing that cancer appeared in higher than expected frequency among such individuals. Retrospective studies of course are exposed to many difficulties (Fox, 1978; Sklar and Anisman, 1981), but the findings are remarkably uniform in suggesting the importance of stress in the causation of cancer.

As regards animal studies, there has been some care in differentiating between acute and chronic stress, although it is of course difficult to differentiate between the effects of stress on the primary neoplastic change induced by carcinogens, and on the cellular level, that occur immediately after such transformations have occurred. There is some evidence for the inhibitory effects of chronic stress on tumour induction, but this is evident only if the stress is applied *after* DNBA administration (Newberry *et al.*, 1972, 1976; Pradhan and Ray, 1974; Ray and Pradhan, 1974). When foot shock is *signalled*, Kavetsky, Turkevich, and Balitsky (1966) found that the incidence of spontaneous tumours was increased rather than inhibited, and Newberry *et al.* (1972) also found that the inhibitory effects of chronic shock were reduced if the stress was signalled. Sklar and Anisman believe that stress predictability may be an important factor in determining the tumorigenic effects of stress, but regard any such conclusion as highly provisional in the present state of ignorance.

The many studies on the effects of acute and chronic stress on tumour growth have mostly confirmed the results of the effects of stress on tumour induction (e.g. Jamasbi and Nettsheim, 1977; Peters, 1975; Peters and Kelly, 1977; Marsh, Miller, and Lamson, 1959; Newberry *et al.*, 1972; Pradhan and Ray, 1974; Nieburgs *et al.*, 1979). These studies all dealt with the *inhibitory* effects of shock on tumour growth; other stressors have been found to have similar effects (e.g. Gershben *et al.*, 1974; Molomut *et al.*, 1963; Pradhan and Ray, 1974; Newberry *et al.*, 1976; Nieburgs *et al.*, 1979; Pradhan and Ray, 1974).

Sklar and Anisman (1981) point out that: 'In addition to the inhibitory effects of chronic stress on tumour cell proliferation (Newberry, 1978) it seems that adaptation to the effects of the stressor may occur with repeated exposure.' (p. 378). They give an example from their own work to show that a single session of inescapable shock, administered 24 hours after transplantation, enhanced the growth of P815 mastocytoma; however, in mice that had previously been exposed to shock for either four or nine days preceding cell transplantation, the effects of subsequent acute stress were eliminated. 'These data appear to indicate that adaptation to stress occurs at some level in the physiological process that governs stress-induced tumorigenic changes.' (p. 378).

In viewing these results it is always necessary to keep in mind the background conditions in which an experimental stressor is applied. When conditions related to animal maintenance are stressful (as indexed by plasma corticosterone levels), experimental stressors may have little effect on tumour development. However, if mice are reared in a more protected environment, tumour-enhancing effects of the stressor are manifested. At the other end, Nieburgs *et al.* (1979) have reported that immunological changes ordinarily provoked by physical stress were not evident among animals that had recently been exposed to stress in the form of transportation from the breeding farm.

As regards metastases, it seems that acute stress may exacerbate metastases, but under conditions of chronic shock administration, the formation and growth of metastases was inhibited (Zimel *et al.* 1977), very much in the way that chronic stress inhibited the induction and growth of primary tumours.

How does emotional, psychosocial, or anxiety-stimulated stress influence the growth of neoplasia? It is well known that such stress produces increased plasma concentration of adrenal corticoids and other hormones through well-known neuroendocrine pathways (Riley, 1981). It is well known that these corticoid concentrations injure elements of the immunological apparatus, and this may leave the subject vulnerable to the action of latent oncogenic viruses, newly transformed cancer cells, or other incipient pathological processes that are normally held in check by an intact immunological apparatus. Riley (1981) describes studies supporting the view that increased plasma concentrations of adrenal corticoids have adverse effects on the thymus and thymus-dependent T cells, i.e. elements which constitute the major defence system against various neoplastic processes and other pathologies. These studies also show that anxiety-stress can be quantitatively induced, and the consequences measured through specific biochemical and cellular effects, always provided that proper baselines of these conditions are obtained in the experimental animals by the use of low-stress protective housing and handling techniques.

Summarizing their much more extensive review of the literature, Sklar and Anisman (1981) report that there appears to be a remarkable parallel among the stress effects on neurochemical, hormonal, and immunological functioning: 'Acute stress results in depletion of catecholamines and increases of ACh, increased synthesis and secretion of hormones, and immuno-suppresion. Adaptation in these biological mechanisms is observed with chronic stress, such that normal levels of functioning or alterations opposite to those induced by acute stress are apparent.' (p. 391). They go on to consider biochemical and other causes for these effects, but it would take us too far to enter into a discussion of these. Let us merely note that there is some evidence that acute stress produces tumour *growth*, chronic stress tumour *reduction*. We may perhaps call this effect an 'inoculation effect'; it is as if the previous experience of stress inoculates the animal against subsequent stress, making it less effective, or even reversing the biological changes produced.

The inoculation or desensitization effect of stress

This inoculation effect is of course well known in experimental psychology (Gray *et al.*, 1981). Consider some defining experiments (e.g. Brown and Wagner, 1964). Two groups of rats are studied in a situation where they are trained to run an alley for food reward. One group is given continuous reinforcement, the other also receives electric shocks, initially of low intensity, but gradually increasing in intensity on successive trials. In the next phase of the experiment, both groups are given reward together with a high-intensity shock on every trial. Comparing the two groups, it is usually found that the group which previously received shock shows much less reluctance to go to food-plus-shock than does the group that did not receive shock.

Another paradigm is that of 'learned helplessness' (Seligman, Maier, and Solomon, 1971). Here one group of rats is given a single session in which it is exposed to inescapable electric shock; it is then trained in a task in which it is again shocked, but in which it is possible to escape from or avoid the shock by jumping from side to side of a two-compartment apparatus known as a 'shuttle-box'. A control group, without exposure to the initial inescapable shocks, is also tested in the shuttle-box. The group with the 'learned helplessness' experience is worse at escaping from shock in the shuttle-box than the control group. However, if the experiment is now repeated with the 'learned helplessness' group given 15 daily sessions of inescapable shock before the shuttle-box test, such animals are just as good at learning to escape shock as the controls. As Gray *et al.* (1981) point out: 'Repeated exposure to inescapable shocks allows the animal to overcome the deleterious effects of a single session of inescapable shock.' Miller (1976) has termed this effect 'toughening up' (see also Weiss and Glaser, 1975; Weiss *et al.*, 1975). The same authors have also reported a similar experiment, identical to the one mentioned above, except that, in place of the inescapable shock sessions, the rats were made to swim in cold water for three to four minutes before the shuttle-box test session. Like inescapable shock, this treatment impairs shuttle-box performance, and also like inescapable shock, fifteen consecutive daily sessions of 'cold swim' overcome the initial deficit, so that shuttle-box performance tested after the final swim is normal.

Gray (1975) has shown that 'frustrative non-reward' can also be used as a stressor, very much like shock or 'cold swim'. Like these other stressors, frustrative non-reward elicits a rise in plasma corticosterone (Goldman, Coover, and Levine, 1973). This technique has been used in experiments similar to those listed above, where again two groups of rats are trained to run in an alley for food reward. One is the control or continuous reinforcement group; the second is trained with a partial reinforcement schedule. In the test phase of the experiment, the simple extinction paradigm is used, and it is found that the experimental group continues to run to the now-empty goal box much more persistently than the control group (Lewis, 1960).

As Gray *et al.* (1981) summarize these findings: 'In each of these four experiments the animal is exposed repeatedly to a stressor (shock, non-reward, cold swim) and comes in consequence to show reduced behavioural responses to the stressor. In these cases, then, the animal develops tolerance for the stressor to which it is exposed.' (p. 154).

Experiments disclose not only direct tolerance effects, as outlined above, but also give evidence of cross-tolerance. Thus exposure to the punishment schedule gives rise to increased resistance to extinction, and conversely, exposure to a partial reinforcement schedule gives rise to increased resistance to punishment (Brown and Wagner, 1964). Exposure to repeated inescapable shock can also be shown to lead to increased resistance to extinction (Chen and Amsel, 1977). In addition, Weiss *et al.* (1975) have shown that repeated exposure to shock prevents cold swim from impairing shuttle-box performance, and repeated exposure to cold swim prevents inescapable shock from having this effect. 'Thus cross-tolerance has been demonstrated in both directions for the pairs, shock and non-reward, shock and cold swim; the pair, non-reward and cold swim does not appear to have been investigated as yet.' (Gray *et al.* 1981, p. 154). Gray *et al.* (1981) report research into possible neuromechanisms for stress tolerance of this kind, but it would take us too far to go into these complex matters here. Let us merely end this section by drawing attention to the close similarities of these experiments and those discussed in the previous section, in supporting the existence of 'inoculation effect'.

Personality

A lengthy discussion of the relationship between personality and cancer has been given by Eysenck (1980), who begins the discussion with the paper by Kissen and Eysenck (1962), reporting an experiment in which 116 male lung cancer patients and 123 non-cancer controls were tested with the Eysenck MPI, both groups being patients at surgical and medical chest units tested *before* diagnosis. The control group was found to have much higher neuroticism scores than the cancer group; this was true equally of subjects with and those without psychosomatic involvement. As regards extraversion, a difference appeared only in the group with psychosomatic disorder, with the cancer group considerably more extraverted than the control group.

In a more recent study, Berndt, Günther, and Rohte (1980), using Eysenck's EPI questionnaire, compared control groups of patients with patients who after completion of the questionnaire were found to suffer from breast cancer or bronchial carcinoma. The size of the female control group was 953; that of the breast cancer group was 231. The male control group numbered 195, and the male bronchial carcinoma group 123. The female bronchial carcinoma group was very small, numbering only 20, which makes it almost impossible for this group to give significant differences from the controls.

As Eysenck (1981b) has shown, in all three groups the cancer patients had neuroticism scores *lower* than the controls, with the differences reaching a $P<.01$ level for the breast cancer group, and the male bronchial carcinoma group; for the female bronchial carcinoma group, because of the small number of patients, the result, although in the same direction, was not statistically significant.

Berndt and his colleagues did not find any significant differences for extraversion, but Hagnell (1962), reporting on the results of an epidemiological survey of the 2515 inhabitants of two adjacent rural parishes in the south of Sweden, found that a significantly high proportion who had developed cancer had been originally rated as extraverted, in a long-term (10 year) follow-up study. Coppen and Metcalfe (1963), using the MPI for their enquiry, compared various cancer groups with two control groups and discovered that the cancer group had significantly higher extraversion scores than both control groups. They failed to find a significant correlation with neuroticism.

Kissen (1964a, 1964b, 1966) took up the relationship between lung cancer and lack of neuroticism which appeared in the Kissen and Eysenck (1962) paper, and again found that lung cancer patients had very significantly lower N scores than did control patients. Kissen gives a rather interesting table in which he calculates lung cancer mortality rates per 100 000 men aged 25 and over by levels of neuroticism scores. He found that people with very low scores had a mortality rate of 296, those with intermediate scores had a mortality rate of 108, and those with very high scores had a mortality rate of only 56. When it is realized that these are all raw figures, i.e. uncorrected for attenuation due to a lack of perfect reliability and validity of the scales, it will be seen that there is considerable support here for the assumption of a strong relationship between the development of lung cancer and constitutional personality factors. In his further work, Kissen (1968) also found some support for the hypothesis that extraversion is more frequent in lung cancer patients, but the trend is rather weak.

Other papers quoted by Eysenck (1980) are those by Abse *et al.* (1974), Ure (1969), Greer and Morris (1975), and many others; as far as they go, these give results in a similar direction to those already reviewed.

Another line or research, also discussed in detail by Eysenck (1980), suggests a negative link between cancer and psychosis, supporting an hypotheses suggested by the title of the Bahnson and Bahnson (1964) paper: 'Cancer is an alternative to psychosis'. Several such studies in different countries are reviewed by Eysenck, dealing with many thousands of cases, and on the whole the hypothesis seems to be well established. We will here only note this curious relationship, without entering into further discussion.

The stress–personality theory

How can we account for the relationship between neuroticism (and psychosis), and absence of malignant tumours? At first sight one might think that if life stress is related to tumour formation, and neuroticism leads to higher strain values for equal stress values, then the opposite kind of relationship would have been expected. Similarly for extraversion; it is the introvert who usually conditions to anxiety-provoking stimuli better than the extravert, and hence is more liable to develop dysthymic neuroses (Eysenck, 1977). Thus both these somewhat oversimplified predictions would seem to go in the wrong direction.

However, such predictions would leave out of account the opposite relationships with tumour production given by acute and chronic stress. We might postulate that high N scorers, even when encountering a similar set of stress-producing stimuli, suffer more *chronic* strain than low N scorers, even when exposure to stressful stimuli is equated. Under these conditions one would expect, on the basis of the evidence reviewed, that high N scorers and introverts would show the 'inoculation effect', and hence be protected to some extent from stresses through the experience of previous high strain.

Much the same might be said about psychotic, particularly schizophrenic and manic depressive, patients. They too will have experienced a high degree of chronic stress in the past (much greater than most normal people), and would consequently benefit from the same inoculation effect. Indeed, for psychotics the effect should be even stronger, because the experience of stressful stimuli to which they have been exposed would be much greater. Thus the inoculation effect forms the mediating link between stress and personality effects in cancer production.

This hypothesis is of course quite different to that proposed by Kissen and others. Following some vague and unconvincing psychodynamic reasoning, they suggest that what characterizes the cancer-prone personality is the *repression* of emotion, and its denial. The absence of high N scores in cancer-prone patients is interpreted as supporting this hypothesis, but there is nothing in the data to justify such an interpretation of the low N scores of cancer patients. The more usual interpretation of low N scores is simply the absence of strong emotional response, and a lack of affect; the interpretation in terms of repression and denial would require separate empirical support, which has not yet been forthcoming.

Admittedly such an hypothesis as that advanced by Kissen is difficult to test empirically, but recent work summarized by Gudjonsson (1982), and his own experiments, show that it is possible by means of specially devised experiments, and also on the basis of questionnaires, to discriminate between 'repressors' and 'sensitizers'. On such questionnaires as the EPQ (Eysenck and Eysenck, 1975), the former have a *high* lie score and a low neuroticism score, while the latter would have a *low* lie score and a *high* neuroticism score. An application of the EPQ to selected groups of cancer patients, as compared with non-cancer patients, would seem to be capable of deciding between the two hypotheses of Kissen, on the one hand, and Eysenck, on the other. On the former hypotheses, the low N score of the cancer patients should be accompanied by unusually high L scores, while according to the latter's hypothesis low N scores should be accompanied by average L scores. Even better would be a replication of the Gudjonsson experiment, using physiological measures, in order to test whether or not the cancer-prone group was indeed made up largely by 'repressors'. Unfortunately no such experiment has been performed, and hence both theories are still viable. It should be noted, however, that while the Eysenck hypothesis links up in a meaningful manner with what is known about the effects of stress, particularly the differentiation between acute and chronic stress, the Kissen hypothesis suggests no causal mechanism, and remains wedded to a purely speculative Freudian type of analysis.

An animal analogue

There are obvious difficulties in testing hypotheses such as those mentioned above, particularly the 'inoculation' hypothesis, on humans, and it may be useful to have an animal analogue. Such an analogue is of course difficult to provide with respect to personality, but research on the specially bred Maudsley Reactive and Non-reactive strains (Broadhurst, 1975; Broadhurst and Eysenck, 1965; Eysenck and Broadhurst, 1964) has shown that rats can be bred for emotionality, and that the trait of 'emotionality' corresponds in many ways quite closely with that of 'neuroticism' in humans. It would seem possible, therefore, to combine personality, stress, and liability to cancer in experiments using animals as subjects. (Savage and Eysenck, 1964).

Only one such experiment appears to have been carried out, by the writer in collaboration with Dr. H. C. Holland and Professor E. A. Wright (unpublished). This experiment used 180 animals of the Maudsley Reactive (MR) and Maudsley Non-reactive (MNR) strains of rats in six treatment groups, each containing 15 males and 15 females. The six groups were made of three 2-value variables, in all possible combinations, namely MR and MNR; stressed and non-stressed; and implanted and not implanted. The stress in the experiment took the form of a mild electric shock to the feet at an intensity of 0.25 mA for 0.7 seconds, administered at a frequency of 12 times per day, i.e. approximately every two hours at an interval which varied between 1½ and 2½ hours. Implantation refers to the use of a carcinogenic agent, a small pellet (approximately 3 mm) of 3-4-Benzpyrene, implanted subdermally under light anaesthesia and located in the flank of the organism by the use of a trocar. The implantation took place at 50 days of age and at the same time as ear-marking. The trocar puncture was closed by a single suture, and following the operative procedure a recovery period of 14 days was allowed before the animal was again handled. The animals were weighed at the time of marking/implantation and, following the recovery period, were weighed every week. Tumour size was recorded as a weekly weighing, the measurement being taken with a modified Harpenden skinfold caliper.

The weighing and measuring process continued until the animal was one year old, or until the tumour produced by the chemical implantation reached a size of 3 cm along a lateral axis, whichever was the earlier. The animal was then sacrified by ether euthanasia with a comparable member of the control group (two experimental animals to one control of the same age, sex, and strain). After death, subjects were autopsied and examination of several organs and glands was conducted (i.e. heart, liver, kidney, spleen, etc.).

Table 1   Outline of analyses of variance of scores (main effects and interaction) representing days from implantation) representing days from implantation of carcinogen to tumour size of 1 cm (including skin thickness in caliper measurement)

Group means (days)

Group 1	(i)	$N=13$ MR	males	(stressed)	170.9
	(ii)	$N=13$ MR	females	(stressed)	183.2
Group 2	(iii)	$N=15$ MNR	males	(stressed)	180.5
	(iv)	$N=9$ MNR	females	(stressed)	176.8
Group 3	(v)	$N=14$ MR	males	(unstressed)	157.4
	(vi)	$N=11$ MR	females	(unstressed)	212.9
Group 4	(vii)	$N=14$ MNR	males	(unstressed)	168.6
	(viii)	$N=11$ MNR	females	(unstressed)	189.1

Analysis of variance outline

Source	df	S.qs.	M.S.V.	VE	p
Between strains	1	30.59	30.59	—	
stress	1	65.61	65.61	—	
sex	1	11 169.04	11 169.04	4.3202	.05
Strains × stress	1	261.36	261.36	—	
Strains × sex	1	3 491.81	3 491.81	1.3506	NS
Stress × sex	1	6 968.11	6 968.11	2.6953	NS
Strains × stress × sex	1	1 031.86	1 031.86	—	
Residual	92	237 848.37	2 585.31		
	99	260 866.75			

Tumour aggressivity was evaluated by counting the number of days taken by members of the different treatment groups to produce tumours of 1, 2, and 3 cm (measured along a lateral axis). The resulting values were then subjected to an analysis of variance in order to outline the systematic differences between sexes, strain, and stress, as well as their first- and second-order interactions. Table 1 shows the results of the analysis; it will be seen that the only factor to refute the null hypothesis at an acceptable level is sex.

A similar analysis was performed for a growth index, defined as:

$$\frac{\text{weight of animal at 134 days minus weight of animal at 50 days}}{\text{average of all weekly weighings from 64 days to 134 days}}$$

Table 2 shows the means and standard deviations for the six groups, and Table 3 shows the analysis of variance carried out on the data.

Table 2   Growth Index for Treatment Groups

Group 1	(implanted, MR, stressed)	mean = 0.509	s.d. = 0.10074
Group 2	(implanted, MNR, stressed)	mean = 0.466	s.d. = 0.13322
Group 3	(implanted, MR, unstressed)	mean = 0.526	s.d. = 0.13892
Group 4	(implanted, MNR, unstressed)	mean = 0.515	s.d. = 0.12806
Group 5	(control)	mean = 0.455	s.d. = 0.16186
Group 6	(control)	mean = 0.477	s.d. = 0.17804

Table 3   Growth Index

Outline of analysis of variance

Source	df	S. Squares	M.S.V.	V.R.	p
Between sex (s)	1	1.542 901	1.542 901	121.5562	.001
Between treatments (T)	2	.041 810	.020 905	1.6470	NS
Between strains (ST)	1	.002 047	.002 047	.1613	NS
Interactions $S \times T$	2	.039 386	.019 693	1.5515	NS
Interactions $S \times ST$	1	.085 849	.085 849	6.7635	.001
Interactions $T \times ST$	2	.105 691	.052 846	4.1634	.05
Interactions $S \times T \times ST$	2	2.218 128	1.109 064	87.3767	.001
Residual	168	2.132 410	.012 693		
Total	179	6.168 222			

Means for Significant Main Effect and Interactions of Outline of Analysis of Variance

Treatment	MR M	F	MNR M	F		M	F	Treatment	MR	MNR
1	.613	.405	.587	.344	MR	.540	.398	1	.509	.466
2	.614	.404	.631	.398	MNR	.590	.361	2	.442	.515
3	.526	.386	.552	.341				3	.456	.447
$\bar{X}$	.584	.398	.590	.361	$\bar{X}$	.565	.380	$\bar{X}$	.469	.476

There is again a highly significant difference due to sex, i.e. differences in the growth rate in males and females, which carried over into a first-order interaction between 'sex' and 'temperament'. The other first-order interaction to reach a suitable confidence level is between 'treatment' and 'strain', and suggests that the reactive strain was more affected by the implantation procedure, but less affected by the addition of electric shock than the non-reactives.

Compared against the residual variance, a highly significant second-order effect was found between strains, treatments, and sex, at the .001 level. As the interactions suggest, different sexes respond differently to different treatments depending on their strain, a finding which, although limited, does suggest that if body weight in any form is to be considered as an indication or as a feature of a pathological process, the strain and the sex of the animals, and indirectly the 'personality' and sex of the animal, are not unimportant constitutional variables which should be considered in conjunction with the nature of any surgical procedure envisaged.

The experiment is quoted, not so much because it throws any direct light on the proposed 'inoculation effect', but because it illustrates the way in which analogue experiments in this field can be conducted. Clearly it will be necessary to carry out many variations in the parameter values before we can hope to achieve positive, replicable results to test the hypothesis adequately. However, in view of the importance of the issue, it is to be hoped that such studies will be carried out in the future, using the reactive and non-reactive strains of rats to test personality effects.

Cardiovascular Disease

Type A–type B behaviour

In the field of cardiovascular disorders, the most widely known and studied relationship is between this type of disorder and Type A–type B behaviour. Dunbar (1959) originally described coronary-prone personality types as striving, ambitious, and authority seeking. Friedman and Rosenman (1959) reported in their coronary patients competitive and intense striving for achievement. They also found an over-commitment to work, corresponding to Dunbar's description of the coronary personality as hard-working. Friedman and Rosenman additionally described in such people a sense of time urgency, impatience, and hostility. Dunbar's description also refers to these more aggressive social characteristics, but sees them as being suppressed or diverted into a socially acceptable competitiveness. The concept of the coronary-prone type A behaviour, which grew from these sources, is characterized by aggressiveness, ambition, competitiveness, time urgency, impatience, behavioural alertness and intense commitment to vocational goals (Rosenman and Chesney, 1980; Steptoe, 1981). There is some evidence for a correlation between these personality characteristics and cardiovascular disease, but there are also major criticisms.

One obvious criticism relates to the meaningfulness of the concept of type A–type B behaviour (Eysenck and Fulker, 1982). Psychologists have abandoned the notion of a *typology*; practically all personality traits are normally distributed, and it seems unlikely that type A behaviour could differ so fundamentally from all other personality traits. Statements that a certain percentage of a given population (varying usually from 50% to 70%) is of type A, are as meaningless as statements that a certain proportion of a population is tall; the implication of a U-shaped distribution, or even a categorical distinction between two 'types', is inherently improbable.

Allied to this criticism is another one, to the effect that concepts should not be put forward without good evidence that the pattern of intercorrelations implicit in the proposed trait or type is actually found; thus it may be that some of the alleged component traits of type A do intercorrelate positively, while others may not. The factorial support for the concept is weak, and the decomposition into three major factors (hard-driving competitiveness; job involvement; speed and impatience) by Jenkins, Zyzanski, and Rosenman (1971) suggests that possibly certain aspects of type A behaviour may be related to coronary heart disease, while others are not.

Actually, many aspects of type A behaviour seem to be related to major dimensions of personality long since recognized by psychologists, particularly extraversion and neuroticism. Lovallo and Pishkin (1980) and Rim (1981) have shown that Bortner's rating scale (Bortner, 1969) correlates significantly with both E and N, and Kornitzer *et al.* (1975; personal communication) found quite high correlations with neuroticism, but not with extraversion.

Eysenck and Fulker (1982) have shown by means of a factor analysis of their own questionnaire of type A–type B behaviour that there are three major factors to be found there which they labelled tenseness, ambition, and activity. These three factors appeared equally for males and females, and *extraversion* was found to correlate quite highly with both ambition and activity, while *neuroticism* correlated even more highly with tenseness. Extraversion and neuroticism are of course uncorrelated, and so were the type A behaviour patterns correlating with these two major dimensions of personality respectively. As Eysenck and Fulker conclude: 'It is clear that the factors emerging from our study of type A behaviour can be largely accounted for in terms of the major dimensions of personality, neuroticism and extraversion, with total type A score lying in the high N–high E quadrant.'

Eysenck and Fulker also looked at the heritability of the three components of the A type. The raw heritabilities ranged around .4, but corrected for attenuation they accounted for about two-thirds of the total variance, leaving only one-third for environmental factors. This agrees well with the know heritabilities of extraversion and neuroticism. (Similar values of heritability have been found by Koskenvuo *et al.*, 1979.)

Eysenck and Fulker (1982) conclude that:

> The best description of the behaviour of our subjects, as far as type A-related traits are concerned, is in terms of E and N; added to this must be specific groups of traits identified in terms of our three factors derived from the factor analysis of type A behaviour. In this general description, it will be noted, there is no trace remaining of the concept of type A behaviour as such; the concept has been shown to be a chimera, stemming from perfectly correct observations of the originators of the concept, followed by psychometrically inappopriate analyses and disregard of much better established personality dimensions.

Personality and disease

When we now turn to the actual relationship between personality and cardiovascular disease, the evidence seems to unearth a rather curious dichotomy. In both retrospective and prospective studies, workers seem to have established a positive correlation between type A behaviour (i.e. neuroticism and extraversion) and cardiovascular disease (Steptoe, 1981), but when we turn to hospitalized patients, the picture is rather different. Bass, in a study quoted by Eysenck and Fulker (1982), studied three groups of patients, the first of which ($N = 30$) complained of angina but were cleared of actual cardiac damage. The second group ($N = 16$) showed signs of slight cardiac disease, and a third group ($N = 53$) was seriously affected by cardiovascular impairments and required surgery. Bass gave all subject a thorough psychiatric morbidity interview, the Eysenck Personality Questionnaire and the Bortner Type A questionnaire. The results showed the first group (no heart disease) to have the highest psychiatric morbidity, high scores on E and N, and the highest scores on the A type behaviour questionnaire. The intermediate group with some cardiac impairment had the next highest psychiatric morbidity, the highest E score of all groups, and medium A-type scores. The group with serious cardiac disease scored *lowest* on psychiatric morbidity, on E and N, and on the A-type behaviour.

Since high E and N scorers have been linked with the 'complainer' syndrome, it seems likely that these same characteristics apply to A types, but that these are not necessarily the patients who subsequently have heart attacks. The A type appears more to describe those patients complaining of chest pains, but who have no physical heart defects, and whose symptoms can be due to psychosomatic disorders, especially hyperventilation, than those patients who are prone to actual coronaries. Other authors have also noted that in groups referred to cardiac units, severity of disorder is *negatively* correlated with type A behaviour, however assessed (Dimsdale *et al.*, 1978; Ahnve *et al.*, 1979). These results are so directly counter to the original hypotheses which led to the development of the typology that they must throw considerable doubt on their adequacy. Clearly much further research will have to be done to establish the precise nature of the relationships between cardiovascular disease and personality.

In this type of research one should also be open to the possibility that different types of cardiovascular disease may be related to different type of personality. Thus Floderus (1974) suggests, and provides some evidence for the suggestion, that angina pectoris, hypertension, and tachicardia may be related to high neuroticism and introversion, while myocardial infarction and hyperlipidemia may be related to high neuroticism and extraversion; the relationship between extraversion and myocardial infarction has been demonstrated by Bendine and Groen (1963). Many other studies (e.g. Baer *et al.*, 1979; Frankenhauser, Lundbert, and Forsman, 1980; Innes, 1980; Jenkins *et al.*, 1977; and Nowak and Sassenrath, 1980) clearly indicate the relevance of N and E to the assessment of different types of coronary-prone behaviour.

The inoculation hypothesis

The findings of Bass, Dimsdale *et al.*, and Ahnve *et al.*, of an inverse relationship between N and E (or type A behaviour) and coronary heart disease may provide an explanation along the same lines as the inverse relationship between neuroticism and cancer, i.e. in terms of a lessening in strain experienced by people exposed to more frequent stressful situations. Given that high N scorers are more likely to experience severe strain than low N scorers, under identical situations, this would render high N scorers less susceptible to stress and strain, and hence less liable to cardiovascular disease. The adequacy of such a theory would of course depend crucially on the hypothetical involvement of stress in the causation of cardiovascular disease. Here the evidence is positive, but not very extensive. It has been found, for instance, that widows suffer an above-average mortality rate in the first five years after bereavement, and much of this is accounted for by cardiovascular disease (Parkes, Benjamin, and Fitzgerald, 1969). When men of 40 to 60 years of age who had recently suffered a heart attack were compared with a matched control group, they showed a significantly high incidence of divorce, and a tendency to report more frequent loss of close friends (Thiel, Parker, and Bruce, 1973). Other studies have suggested that heart disease is common in those who have emigrated (Medalie *et al.*, 1973).

In addition to these studies, it is necessary to bear in mind the points made at the beginning of this chapter, namely that identical stresses may produce different strains in different personalities. Thus Suls, Gastorf and Witenberg (1979) found that students with a high type A score reported more life events of a stressful character than those with the opposite personality features. It is also found that type A students were particularly disturbed by events that they saw as undesirable, unexpected, or ambiguous in terms of their perceived control over them. Type B students, on the other hand, became less distressed the more they perceived the events as out of their personal control. The implication of course is that type A individuals, with their need to control events, have greater difficulties in falling back on external support even when this is clearly desirable and available. It is clearly not sufficient to list stresses without some direct knowledge of the strain produced in different types of personality. That the type of external support mentioned above is important, particularly when it is of a social kind, is shown by a report of the Human Population Laboratory Survey, using a random sample of 7000 adults aged 20 years or over (Berkman and Syme, 1979). Looking at four sources of social contact (marriage, contact with close friends, church membership, and informal and formal group associations), they found that mortality rate was clearly related to the total quantity of social support. Intimate contact, as one might have expected, had greater weight in this connection than less intimate. This type of social influence was found to make a contribution to relative absence of heart disease and cancer.

The 'inoculation' hypothesis does not apply as clearly in the field of coronary heart disease as it does in the cancer field, but this may be more apparent than real in view of the relative poverty of relevant experimental material. At the very least, it supplies a testable *causal* theory to supplant the purely descriptive type A–type B hypothesis, which in any case is open to considerable criticism. Even at the descriptive level more than that cannot be claimed for it at the present time.

Conclusion

We have seen that the relationship between personality, stress, and disease (using cancer and cardiovascular disease in our paradigms) is very complex, and that it is difficult to come to any kind of definitive conclusions. However, gradually it would seem that certain relationships are appearing which are replicable, understandable, and may lead to a better interpretation of these very complex factors. Disregarding all the necessary qualifications, some of which have been introduced in the course of the preceding discussion, we may perhaps recapitulate the major point of the theory here developed in terms of a number of sequential points.

1. The concept of *stress* cannot be understood without reference to *strain*, the former being the stimulus, objectively measurable and identical for

all individuals, and the latter being the response of a given individual, frequently different from one individual to another.

2. The relationship between stress and strain can only be understood in terms of a system of *individual differences*, the more important of which in this relation being neuroticism–stability and extraversion–introversion.

3. It seems possible to trade personality against severity of stress, in the sense that identical stresses produce greater strain in high N (and possibly low E) subjects, so that equal strain may be achieved by administering less stressful situations to high N subjects, etc.

4. Stress seems to be causally related to cancer, but in opposite directions depending on whether the stress is *acute* or *chronic*.

5. Acute stress produces an *incrementation* in the production of cancerous growths, whereas chronic stress appears to have the reverse effect.

6. The beneficial effects of chronic stress on the production of carcinomas may be labelled the 'inoculation effect' by analogy with well-known medical processes. The applicability of the analogy, of course, still awaits experimental documentation.

7. Because of the greater strain suffered under identical conditions of stressful exposure, high N (and possible low E) subjects would be expected to show a greater inoculation effect as opposed to low N (and possibly high E) subjects.

8. On this basis one would predict that carcinomas would be more readily found in individuals low on N, and/or high on E, and the evidence gives substantial support for this prediction.

9. Similarly, it would be predicted that psychotic individuals, suffering from the more common forms of functional psychosis, would be relatively free of cancer, in view of the inoculation qualities of the severe stress experienced in everyday life. This has always been found to be so in empirical studies.

10. Cardiovascular disease, too, has been found to be affected by life stress.

11. As a consequence, similar predictions to those made for cancer can be made in the field of cardiovascular disease.

12. Relationships between N and E, on the one hand, and cardiovascular disease on the other, are complex; there seems to be a direct relationship with N, and possibly E, as far as general population studies are concerned. This would be counter to prediction.

13. However, in studies of *clinical populations* suffering or not suffering from coronary heart disease, the expected relationship between N and disease has been found, in the sense that those least subject to the disease were found to have the highest N scores.

Clearly the theory here offered, while explaining some of the observed relationships, is in urgent need of more direct empirical support. Alternative theories exist, and have been discussed in some detail. They do not lend themselves so readily to empirical investigation, but methods now exist for some form of crucial experiment. It is to be hoped that such experiments will soon be carried out to decide between these alternative hypotheses. What probably cannot be doubted any longer is the relevance of both personality and stress in the causation and maintenance of carcinoma and cardiovascular disease. The details of the interrelationships between these variables are almost certainly more complex than suggested here, and will take a long time to unravel. However, a beginning has been made in making more precise the relationships that may exist in this field, and the hypotheses advanced, whether right or wrong, at least fulfil the minimum requirement of a scientific hypothesis, namely that of being testable. Their main value may be the heuristic one of directing research along certain promising paths; it seems unlikely that any of the existing theories will survive empirical testing for a very long period of time without being altered in many important directions. What is unlikely to happen, however, is a disproof of the hypothesis that personality and stress, in combination, are relevant to the development of cancers, cardiovascular disease, and many other disorders not perhaps normally regarded as psychosomatic (Eysenck, 1981a).

It would be interesting to speculate upon the possible interaction effects of smoking with stress and personality, as independent variables, on cancer and CHD as dependent variables, but it must be doubtful if enough information is available to make such a venture worth while. Existing knowledge in the fields relating to the causes and effects of smoking is limited, particularly insofar as connections with cancer and CHD are concerned (Eysenck, 1980), and research workers have seldom considered the complex interactions with stress and personality clearly relevant to any sophisticated appraisal of possible cigarette-smoking effects. Research at a more complex level is urgently needed if these interactions are to be properly understood. In the absence of such research, speculations would be distinctly premature.

References

Abse, D. W., Wilkins, M. M., Castle, R., Buxton, W. D., Demars, J., Brown, R. S., and Kirschner, L. G. (1974) Personality and behavioral characteristics of lung cancer patients. *J. Psychosomat. Res.*, **18**, 101–13.
Ahnve, S.., Faire, U., Orth-Gomer, K., and Theorell, T. (1979) Type-A behaviour in patients with non-coronary chest pain admitted to a coronary care unit. *J. Psychosomat. Res.*, **23**, 219–23.
Baer, P. E., Collins, F. H., Bourianoff, G. G., and Ketchel, M. F. (1979) Assessing personality factors in essential hypertension with a brief self report instrument. *Psychosom. Med.*, **41**, 321–30.
Bahnson, C. B., and Bahnson, M. B. (1964) Cancer as an alternative to psychosis. In D. M. Kissen and I. LeShan (Eds), *Psychosomatic Aspects of Neoplastic Disease.* Philadelphia: Lippincott.

Bendine, J., and Groen, J. (1963) A psychological-statistical study of neuroticism and extraversion in patients with myocardial infarction. *J. Psychosom. Res.*, **7**, 11–14.

Berkman, C. F., and Syme, S. C. (1979) Social networks, lost resistance, and mortality: a nine-year follow-up study of Alameda County residents. *Amer. J. Epidemiol.*, **109**, 186–204.

Berndt, H., Günther, H., and Rothe, G. (1980) Persönlichkeits struktur nach Eysenck bei Kranken mit Brustdrüsen und Bronchialkrebs und Diagnoseverzögerung durch den Patienten. *Arch. f. Geschwülstf.*, **50**.

Bloom, B. L., Asher, S. J., and White, S. W. (1978) Marital disruption as a stressor. A review and analysis. *Psychol. Bull.*, **85**, 867–94.

Bortner, R. W. (1969) A short rating scale as a potential measure of pattern A behavior. *J. Chronic Dis.*, **22**, 87–91.

Broadhurst, P. L. (1975) The Maudsley reactive and non-reactive strains of rats: A survey. *Behav. Genet.*, **5**, 299–319.

Broadhurst, P. L., and Eysenck, H. J. (1965) Emotionality in the rat: A problem of response specificity. In C. Banks and P. L. Broadhurst (Eds), *Studies in Psychology*. University of London Press, 205–21.

Brown, R. T., and Wagner, A. R. (1964) Resistance to punishment and extinction following training with shock or nonreinforcement. *J. Exp. Psychol.*, **68**, 503–7.

Chen, J. S., and Amsel, A. (1977) Prolonged, unsignaled, inescapable shocks increase persistence in subsequent appetitive instrumental learning. *Amin. Learn. Behav.*, **5**, 377–85.

Coppen, A., and Metcalfe, M. (1963) Cancer and extraversion. *Brit. Med. J.*, July 6, 18–19.

Davies, M. H. (1981) Stress, personality, and coronary artery disease. *Brit. J. Hosp. Med.*, 352–60.

Dimsdale, J. E., Hackett, T. P., Hutter, M., Block, D. S., and Catazano, D. (1978) Type A personality and extent of coronary atherosclerosis. *Amer. J. Cardiol.*, **42**, 583–6.

Dunbar, H. F. (1959) *Psychiatry in the Medical Specialities*. New York: McGraw–Hill.

Ernster, V. L., Sacks, T., Selvin, S., and Petrakis, N. C. (1979) Cancer incidence by marital status: U.S. Third National Cancer Survey. *J. Nat. Cancer Inst.*, **63**, 567–85.

Eysenck, H. J. (1967) *The Biological Basis of Personality*. Springfield: C. C. Thomas.

Eysenck, H. J. (1975) The measurement of emotion: Psychological parameters and methods. In, *Emotions: Their Parameters and Measurement*. New York: Raven Press.

Eysenck, H. J. (1976) *The Measurement of Personality*. Lancaster: Medical & Technical Publishers; and Baltimore: University Park Press.

Eysenck, H. J. (1977) *You and Neurosis*. London: Maurice Temple Smith.

Eysenck, H. J. (1980) *The Causes and Effects of Smoking*. London: Maurice Temple Smith; and Los Angeles: Sage.

Eysenck, H. J. (1981a) Personality and psychosomatic diseases. *Act. Nerv. Superior*, **23**, 112–29.

Eysenck, H. J. (1981b) Personality and cancer: some comments on a paper by Berndt, H. *et al. Arch. f. Geschwülstf.*, **51**, 442–3.

Eysenck, H. J., and Broadhurst, P. L. (1964) Experiments with animals. In H. J. Eysenck (Ed.), *Experiments in Emotion*, London: Pergamon Press, 285–91.

Eysenck, H. J., and Eysenck, S. B. G. (1975) *The Manual of the E.P.Q.* London: Hodder and Stoughton.

Eysenck, H. J., and Fulker, D. (1982) The components of Type A behaviour and its genetic determination. *Activ. Nerv. Superior* (in press).

Eysenck, H. J., and Wilson, G. D. (1973) *The Experimental Study of Freudian Theories*. London: Methuen.

Floderus, B. (1974) Psycho-social factors in relation to coronary heart disease and associated risk factors. *Nordisk Hygienisk Tidskrift, Supplementum 6*, Stockholm.

Fox, B. H. (1978) Premorbid psychological factors as related to cancer incidence. *J. Behav. Med.*, **1**, 45–133.

Frankenhauser, M., Lundbert, U., kd Forsman, L. (1980) Note on arousing type A persons by depriving them at work. *J. Psychosom. Res.*, **24**, 45–7.

Friedman, M., and Rosenman, R. H. (1959) Association of specific overt behavior patterns with blood and cardiovascular findings. *J. Amer. Med. Assoc.*, **269**, 1289–96.

Gershben, L. L., Benuck, I., and Shurrager, P. S. (1974) Influence of stress on lesion growth and on survival of animals bearing parenteral and intracerebral leukemia L1210 and Walker tumors. *Oncology*, **30**, 429–435.

Goldman, L., Coover, G. D., and Levine, S. (1973) Bidirectional effects of reinforcement shifts on pituitary adrenal activity. *Physiol. Behav.*, **10**, 209–14.

Gray, J. A. (1975) *Elements of a Two-process Theory of Learning* London Academic Press.

Gray, J. A., Davis, N., Owen, S., Feldon, J., and Boarder, M. (1981) Stress tolerance: possible neural mechanisms. In M. J. Christie and P. G. Millett (Eds), *Psychosomatics*. New York: Wileyand Sons.

Greene, W. A. (1966) The psychosocial setting of the development of leukemia and lymphoma. *Ann. N.Y. Acad. Sci.*, **125**, 794–801.

Greene, W. A., and Swisher, S. N. (1969) Psychological and somatic variables associated with the development and course of monozygotic twins discordant for leukemia. *Ann. N.Y. Acad. Sci.*, **164**, 394–408.

Greer, S., and Morris, T. (1975) Psychological attributes of women who develop breast cancer: A controlled study. *J. Psychosom. Res.*, **19**, 147–53.

Gudjonsson, G. H. (1982) Self-reported emotional disturbance and its relation to electrodermal reactivity, defensiveness and trait anxiety. *Person. & Ind. Diff.* (in press).

Hagnell, O. (1962) *Svenska Laki-Tidu*, **58**, 4928.

Horne, R L. and Picard, R. S. (1979) Psychosocial risk factors for lung cancer. *Psychosom. Med.*, **41**, 503–14.

Innes, J. M. (1980) Impulsivity and the coronary-prone behavior patterns. *Psychol. Rep.*, **47**, 976–8.

Jacobs, T. J., and Charles, E. (1980) Life events and the occurrence of cancer in children. *Psychosom. Med.*, **42**, 11–24.

Jamasbi, R. J., and Nettsheim, P. (1977) Non-immunological enhancement of tumor transplantability in x-irradiated host animals. *Brit. H. Cancer*, **36**, 723–9.

Jenkins, C. D., Zyaanski, S. J., and Rosenman, R. H. (1971) Progress towards validation of a computer-scored test of Type A coronary-prone behavior patterns. *Psychosom. Med.*, **33**, 192–202.

Jenkins, C. D., Zyzanski, S. J., Ryan, T. J., Flessas, A., and Tannenbaum, S. I. (1977) Social insecurity and coronary-prone type A responses as identifiers of severe atherosclerosis. *J. Consult. & Clin. Psychol.*, **45**, 1060–7.

Jensen, A. R. (1962) Extraversion, neuroticism and social learning. *Acta Psychol.*, **20**, 69–77.

Kavetsky, R. E., Turkevich, N. M., and Balitsky, K. P. (1966) On the psychophysiological mechanism of the organism's resistance to tumour growth. *Ann. N.Y. Acad. Sci.*, **125**, 933–45.

Kissen, D. M. (1964a) Relationship between lung cancer, cigarette smoking, inhalation and personality. *Brit. J. Med. Psychol.*, **37**, 203–16.

Kissen, D. M. (1964b) Lung cancer, inhalation and personality. In D. M. Kissen and C. L. LeShan (Eds), *Aspects of Neoplastic Disease*. London: Pitman.

Kissen, D. M. (1966) Psychosocial factors, personality and prevention of lung cancer. *Med. Officer*, **116**, 135–8.

Kissen, D. M. (1968) Some methodological problems in clinical psychosomatic research with special reference to chest disease. *Psychosom. Med.*, **30**, 324–35.

Kissen, D. M., and Eysenck, H. J. (1962) Personality in male lung cancer patients. *J. Psychosom. Res.*, **6**, 123–37.

Kornitzer, M., Kittel, F., Rustin, R. M., Degre, C., Dramaix, M., Debacker, G., and Thilly, C. (1975) Facteurs psychologiques et sociaux en relation avec les cardiopathies ischémiques (C.I.). Données initiales du projet belge de prevention des affections cardiovasculaires. *Archives des Maladies du Coeur et Vaisseaux (Paris)*, **68**, 35–44.

Koskenvuo, M., Langinvainio, H., Kaprio, J., Rautasalo, I., and Sarna, S. (1979) The Finnish Twin Registry: Baseline characteristics. Section 700: occupational and psychosocial factors, *Hensinkin Yliopston Kausanterrej-stieteen*. Helsinki: Laitos.

LeShan, L. L. (1966) An emotional life history pattern associated with neoplastic disease. *Ann. N.Y. Acad. Sci.*, **125**, 780–93.

Lewis, D. J. (1960) Partial reinforcement: a selective review of the literature since 1950. *Psychol. Bull.*, **57**, 1–28.

Lombard, H. L., and Potter, E. A. (1950) Epidemiological aspects of cancer of the cervix: Heriditary and environmental factors. *Cancer*, **3**, 960–8.

Lovallo, W. R., and Pishkin, V. (1980) Type A behavior, self-involvement, autonomic activity, and the traits of neuroticism and extraversion. *Psychosomatic Med.*, **42**, 329–34.

Marsh, J. T., Miller, B. E., and Lamson, B. G. (1959) Effects of repeated brief stress on growth of Ehrlich carcinoma in the mouse. *J. Nat. Cancer Inst.*, **22**, 961–77.

Medalie, J. H., Kahn, H. A., Neufeld, H. N., et al. (1973) Myocardial infarction over a five-year period. I. Prevalence, incidence and mortality experience. *J. Chronic Dis.*, **26**, 63–84.

Miller, N. E. (1976) Learning stress and systematic symptoms. *Acta Neurobiol. Exp.*, **36**, 141–56.

Molomut, N., Lazere, F., and Smith, L. W. (1963) Effect of audiogenic stress upon methylcholanthrene-induced carcinogenesis in mice. *Cancer Research*, **23**, 1097–1101.

Murphy, D. P. (1952) *Heredity in Uterine Cancer*. Cambridge, Mass.: Harvard University Press.

Newberry, B. H. (1978) Restraint-induced inhibition of 7,12-dimethylbenz(a) anthracene-induced mammary tumours: Relation to stages of tumour development. *J. Nat. Cancer Inst.*, **61**, 725–9.

Newberry, B. H., Frankie, B., Beatty, P. A., Maloney, B. D., and Gilchrist, J. C. (1972) Shock stress and DMBA-induced mammary tumours. *Psychosomatic Med.*, **34**, 295–303.

Newberry, B. H., Gildow, J., Wogan, J., and Reese, R. L. (1976) Inhibition of Huggins tumours by force restraint. *Psychosom. Med.*, **38**, 155–62.

Nieburgs, H. E., et al. (1979) The role of stress in human and experimental oncogenesis. *Cancer Detection and Prevention*, **2**, 307–36.

Nowak, K. M., and Sassenrath, J. M. (1980) Coronary-prone behavior, locus of control, and anxiety. *psychol, Rep.*, **47**, 359–64.

Parkes, C. M., Benjamin, B., and Fitzgerald, R. G. (1969) Broken heart: A statistical study of increased mortality among widowers. *Brit. Med. J.*, **1**, 740–3.

Peller, S. (1952) *Cancer in Man*. New York: International Univ. Press.

Peters, L. J. (1975) Enhancement of syngeneic murine tumour transplantation by whole body irradiation — A non-immunological phenomenon. *Brit. J. Cancer*, **31**, 293–300.

Peters, L. J., and Kelly, H. (1977) The influence of stress and stress hormones on the transplantability of a non-immunogenic syngeneic murine tumour. *Cancer*, **39**, 1482–8.

Pradhan, S. N., and Ray, P. (1974) Effects of stress on growth of transplanted and 7,12-dimethylbenz(a) anthracene-induced tumors and their modification by psychotropic drugs. *J. Nat. Cancer Inst.*, **53**, 1241–5.

Ray, P., and Pradhan, S. N. (1974) Growth of transplanted and induced tumors in rats under a schedule of punished behaviors. *J. Nat. Cancer Inst.*, **52**, 575–7.

Riley, V. (1981) Psychoneuroendocrine influences on immuno-competence and neoplasia. *Science*, **217**, 1100–9.

Rim, Y. (1981) Pattern A behaviour and its personality correlates in students of both sexes. *Scientia Paedagog. Experimentalis*, **18**, 98–102.

Rosenbaum, A. (1953) Stimulus generalization as a function of level of experimentally induced anxiety. *J. Exp. Psychol.*, **45**, 35–43.

Rosenbaum, R. (1956) Stimulus generalization as a function of clinical anxiety. *J. Abnorm. Soc. Psychol.*, **53**, 281–5.

Rosenman, R. H., and Chesney, M. A. (1980) The relationship of Type A behavior patterns to coronary heart disease. *Activitas Nerv. Superior*, **22**, 1–45.

Savage, R. D., and Eysenck, H. J. (1964) The definition and measurement of emotionality. In H. J. Eysenck (Ed.), *Experiments in Motivation*. London: Pergamon.

Seligman, M. E. P., Maier, S. F., and Solomon, R. C. (1971) Unpredictable and uncontrollable aversive events. In F. R. Brush (Ed.), *Abersive Conditioning and Learning*. New York: Academic Press, 347–400.

Sklar, L. S., and Anisman, H. (1981) Stress and cancer. *Psychol. Bull.*, **89**, 369–406.

Steptoe, A. (1981) *Psychological Factors in Cardiovascular Disorders*. London: Academic Press.

Suls, J., Gastorf, J. W., and Witenberg, S. H. (1979) Life events, psychological distress and the type of coronary-prone behavior pattern. *J. Psychosom. Res.*, **23**, 315–19.

Thiel, H. G., Parker, D., and Bruce, T. A. (1973) Stress factors and the risk of myocardial infarction. *J. Psychosom. Res.*, **17**, 43–57.

Ure, D. M. (1969) Negative association between allergy and cancer. *Scottish Med. J.*, **14**, 51–4.

Weiss, J. M., Glazer, H. I., Pohorecky, C. A., Brick, J., and Miller, N. E. (1975) Effects of chronic exposure to stressors on avoidance-escape behavior and on brain norepinephrine. *Psychosom. Med.*, **37**, 523–34.

Weiss, J. M., and Glazer, H. I. (1975) Effects of acute exposure to stressors on subsequent avoidance-escape behavior. *Psychosomatic Medicine*, **37**, 499–521.

Zimel, H., Zimel, A., Petrescu, R., Ghinea, E., and Tasca, C. (1977) Influence of stress and of endocrine imbance on the experimental metastasis. *Neoplasma*, **24**, 151–9.

Note:

1. Preparation of this chapter was aided by a special grant from the Council for Tobacco Research, USA, Inc., which also financed the experiment reported in the section entitled 'An animal analogue'. I am indebted to Dr. J. A. Gray for advice and help on various points, to Dr. H. C. Hollund for help with the animal experiment, and to Professor A. Wright for advice on tumour induction.

INDEX

absence of malignant tumours 132
acute and chronic stress on tumour
    growth 127
acute events 53
adaptation 44
adaptation energy 5
adrenal-medullar response 23
adrenocortical activation 23
adrenocorticotrophic hormone 6, 105
adverse life events 111
aetiological role 80
alarm reaction 4
animal studies 127
anticipated fit 47, 48
anxiety-stimulated stress 128
appraisal of an environmental
    situation 81
attribution theory 63
avoidable and unavoidable stress 126

being fired 93
biofeedback 16
biologic stress 2
broken families 97
buffering effect of social support 67

cancer 103
cancer-causing mechanisms 104
cancer and psychosis 131
cancer, stress and personality 126
cardiovascular disease 136
causation and maintenance of
    carcinoma 142
characteristics of the person 27
CHD rates 82

chronic and acute stress 126
chronic conditions 53, 83
clinical populations 141
compartmentalisation of work and home
    life 116
controllability 24
controllability and predictability of life
    events 95
coping 43
coping mechanisms 126
coping styles 29
cross-cultural research 88
cross-resistance 11
cross-sectional and case control
    studies 95
cross-sensitization 11

definition and measurement of
    emotionality 123
denial 109
depression 106
desensitization effect of stress 129
development of cancer in humans 126
differential strain 124
diminished outlet for emotional
    discharge 106
direct effects of strain 52
direct pathogens 14
dual role 116

effects of strain on PE fit 52
employment status and behaviour 112
environmental challenge 27, 30
European Common Market policy
    toward women 117

147

expectancy effects 50
experimental stressors 127
exposure to inescapable shock 129
extraversion 131

fit and strain 38
flexible working arrangements 114
Flexitime 115
frustrative non-reward 129
functional psychosis 141
future of stress research 20

General Adaptation Syndrome (GAS) 4

heterostasis 14
homeostasis 14
hypochondriasis 106

immunity-susceptibility status 83
incidence of coronary heart disease 112
indirect effects of strain 52
indirect pathogens 14
individual differences 141
inhibitory effects of chronic stress 127
inoculation effect 121, 128
inoculation hypothesis 129

job loss 94

learned helplessness 129
life cycle dynamics 86
life events and cancer 108
life events and depression 83
local adaptation syndrome (LAS) 8
longitudinal research designs for
    stressful life experiences 89
loss of a loved person 109

married female executive 112
maternity leave 117
Maudsley Personality Inventory
    (MPI) 124
measurement of PE fit 39
measurement or research design in life
    events 88
mechanism of stress 6
metastases 128
methodological issues in PE fit 68
Midtown Manhattan study 91
model of stress response 24
moderator variables 125

morbidity 82
mother and worker 113
myocardial infarction (MI) 84

needs for a sense of mastery 62
neuroendocrine pathways 128
neuromechanisms for stress
    tolerance 130
neuroticism and extraversion 137
nonspecific adaptive response 2

objective vs. subjective fit 36
occurrence of illness 80
opportunistic study of single events 93

paranoia 106
part time work 115
paternity leave 117
pathogenesis of cancer 110
PE fit theory: 37
    scale contamination 40
    extension 42
Person-Environment Fit 35
personal controllability 63
personal integration 106
personal lifestyle characteristics 86
personality predispositions 105
personality predispositions and
    cancer 106
philosophic implications 17
pluricausal diseases 13
prediction of strain 54
pressures of working women 103
primary and secondary prevention 31
prospective cohort studies 84
prospective research designs 85
psychiatric morbidity 138
psychiatric status and social adjustment
    among women 112
psychosocial epidemiology 81
psychosocial risk factors 82
psychosocial stress and cancer 103
psychosomatic disorders 121

racial discrimination 97
relationship between stress and
    strain 122
relaxation techniques 16
repression 107
repression of emotion 132
repressors and sensitizers 133

response certainty 68
response uncertainty 69
retirement 93
retrospected fit 47
retrospective life-event studies 83

serum cholesterol 92
shock phase 4
SLE-disease orientation 86
slice of life longitudinal design 91
smoking with stress 142
smoothing the way for women 111
stability of objective fit 46
stage of exhaustion 5
stage of resistance 5
stages of disease development 82
strain 46, 140
stress 81
stress and disease 12
stress and working women 111
stress concept 2
stress, disease and personality 121
stress-personality paradigm 121
stress response 9
stressful life experiences 79
stressor 2
stressor situation 26

subjective misfit 62
suicide attempters 96
suppression and denial 29
syntoxic and catatoxic agents 10

theories of human stress 36
time perspective in PE fit 68
trait anxiety 124
Type A behaviour pattern (TABP) 21,
    82, 113, 136
Type A behaviour and sympathetic
    arousal 25
Type B behaviour pattern 24

U-shaped curves 39

ways of maintaining stability of PE
    fit 60
ways to improve PE fit 59
ways to worsen PE fit 60
Western Collaborative Group Study
    (WCGS) 25
what organisations can do 114
work ix
working at home 115
working women 103, 114

Date Due

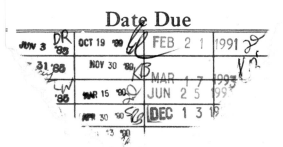